COASTAL NEW ENGLAND WINTERFARE AND HOLIDAY COOKING

Second Edition

By
Sherri Eldridge

Illustrations by
Robert Groves
Nadine Pranckunas

The gratitude of the author is extended to the Maine Chapter of the American Heart Association for the guidance and information provided. The use of the Association's name to convey the goals of this series of books is also gratefully appreciated. For each book sold the publisher makes a contribution to the American Heart Association to further their life-preserving efforts of research and education.

Coastal New England Winterfare & Holiday Cooking
by Sherri Eldridge
Published by Harvest Hill Press

For additional copies of the cookbooks in this series:

Coastal New England Spring Cooking   *Coastal New England Summertime Cooking*
Coastal New England Fall Harvest Cooking   *Coastal New England Winterfare & Holiday Cooking*

send $13.95 per book (Maine residents add state sales tax) plus shipping of $2.00 for the first book and $1.00 for each additional book to the publisher:

Harvest Hill Press, P.O. Box 55, Salisbury Cove, Maine 04672
VISA and Master Card are accepted. Credit card orders may call (207) 288-8900.

ISBN: 1-886862-12-5 (Second Edition)   PRINTED IN THE U.S.A.

First printing: March 1995
Second printing: June 1995 (Revised)
Third Printing: September 1996
Fourth Printing: December 1997 (Second Edition)
Fifth Printing: September 2000

20% TOTAL RECYCLED FIBER
20% POST CONSUMER FIBER

PREFACE

On a cold winter day, hearty recipes created in Coastal New England towns warm households across the nation. Just as the harsh coastal climate brought together the people who made New England their home, the recipes developed by the settlers were shared at sewing bees and socials. Today, we share food and celebration at potluck suppers, in the company of friends and relatives. As New England has become more culturally diverse with every new generation, each has added an interpretation of flavor to expand the coastal New England cuisine.

With the publication of this second edition, a nutritional analysis has been added to help meet your dietary goals. The American Heart Association has developed sound guidelines to assist in the prevention of heart disease, and living a long and healthy life. A pleasurable diet, low in fats and meats, and high in seasonally fresh vegetables, fruits, fish and grains has also been shown to have numerous other health benefits.

These recipes have been adapted to meet the guidelines of the American Heart Association for healthy adults. Although all recipes are reduced in fat and cholesterol, those such as chocolate desserts should not be eaten every day, but enjoyed once or twice a week. A heart-healthy diet includes diverse and good-tasting dishes that are reasonably low in fat, served in average size portions, employing common sense meal plans, and regular exercise.

The Hints and References section has specific guidelines for a heart-healthy diet. Also shown is data on the fats and cholesterol found in oils. Although the sodium and sugars in these recipes have been reduced or removed, people on strict diets should adapt recipes to their individual needs.

Please take a few minutes and explore the resources in this book. It has been carefully written to offer you the best of Coastal New England Cooking.

This book is dedicated to
Eliot Brye,
who showed me that the most
creative and magical kitchen to work in
begins with the least amount of food.

The Coastal New England Cookbook Collection follows the American Heart Association Guidelines for Healthy Adults. These wonderful recipes will help make following the American Heart Association guidelines easier and more fun for you by supplying flavorful reduced fat/salt menu ideas using ingredients from your shelves.

...Beth Davis, R.D. M.Ed.

Beth Davis is a Registered Dietician and former member of the American Heart Association's Speaker's Bureau and Heart Health Education of the Young Task Force.

CREDITS:

Cover: "Canterbury Manor" from cotton print, gratefully used as a courtesy of:
Hoffman International Fabrics

Cover Designs, Layout and Typesetting: Sherri Eldridge

Front Cover Nautical and Back Cover Watercolors, Chapter Title Page Art:
Robert Groves, Brooksville, Maine

Text Line Sketches: Robert Groves and Nadine Pranckunas

Proofreading: Marcie Correa, Bill Eldridge, Eleanor Rhinelander and Ellen Bowlin

Support, Patience and Recipes: Bill Eldridge, Fran Goldberg, The LeForestiers, Annie Shaw and the Women's Business Development Corporation

Coastal New England Winterfare & Holiday

CONTENTS

Breakfast
and
Fresh Fruits

CONTENTS

For other breakfast foods, please refer to the chapters
"Breads and Baked Goods" and "Desserts and Sweets."

Banana-Fruit Smoothie

3 bananas
$^3/_4$ cup drained and
    chopped peaches
    in unsweetened juice
$^1/_2$ cup unsweetened
    applesauce
1 cup non-fat plain
    yogurt
1 cup orange juice
3 tablespoons frozen juice
    concentrate, any kind
$^1/_4$ cup honey
2 teaspoons lemon juice

SERVES 3

Chop bananas into 1-inch pieces. Place all ingredients in blender and whip 1 minute, or until smooth.

Serving: 1/3 Recipe	Calories: 328	Protein: 6 gm
Calories from Fat: 6	Total Fat: .5 gm	Dietary Fiber: 4 gm
Saturated Fat: 0 gm	Carbs: 80 gm	Sodium: 49 mg
Component of Fat: 1%	Cholesterol: 0 mg	Calcium: 123 mg

A Bowl of Ambrosia

A cheery fruit medley to brighten any cold winter morning.

3 large navel oranges
3 ripe bananas
$^1/_2$ cup fresh pineapple
    pieces, or unsweetened
    canned pineapple
$^1/_4$ cup honey or sugar
$^3/_4$ cup shredded coconut
4 tablespoons orange juice
cherries or strawberries
    for garnish (optional)

SERVES 4

Carefully peel and remove membranes from orange sections, leaving sections whole.

Cut bananas into small pieces. Combine bananas with pineapple, honey or sugar, and shredded coconut.

Arrange alternate layers of oranges and banana/pineapple mixture in individual serving dishes. Over the top of each bowl of ambrosia, sprinkle 1 tablespoon orange juice. Chill well before serving. Garnish with a cherry or strawberry.

Serving: 1/4 Recipe	Calories: 258	Protein: 3 gm
Calories from Fat: 51	Total Fat: 5.5 gm	Dietary Fiber: 6 gm
Saturated Fat: 4.5 gm	Carbs: 55 gm	Sodium: 5 mg
Component of Fat: 18%	Cholesterol: 0 mg	Calcium: 51 mg

Broiled Fruits with Spiced Honey

SERVES 4

1 cup raspberry jam
2 teaspoons butter
2 tablespoons honey
1 tablespoon cinnamon
pinch of salt
2 cans fruit: peaches,
     apricots, pineapple
     and/or pears in
     unsweetened juice

Put raspberry jam in small saucepan with butter, honey, cinnamon and salt. Cook for 10 minutes over medium heat, stirring frequently to prevent sticking.

Spray baking pan with non-stick vegetable oil. Place fruits on baking pan (peaches, pears and apricots hollow-side up.) Coat by spooning a thick layer of sauce over each fruit.

Place under broiler, watching closely, until lightly brown. Broiled fruits make a pretty presentation by themselves or over pancakes.

Serving: 1/4 Recipe	Calories: 292	Protein: 1 gm
Calories from Fat: 21	Total Fat: 2.5 gm	Dietary Fiber: 4 gm
Saturated Fat: 1.5 gm	Carbs: 73 gm	Sodium: 88 mg
Component of Fat: 7%	Cholesterol: 5 mg	Calcium: 42 mg

Honey producers in New England are often travelling apiaries. The beekeeper, with his bees and hives, travels from field to field to pollinate different crops. The delicate scent of the blossoms is transmitted to the honey the bees then produce. For example, "blueberry" or "apple" honey has been made by bees while they pollinate those crops.

Chilled Prunes in Wine

1$\frac{1}{2}$ cups dried pitted
    prunes
1 cup water
$\frac{1}{2}$ cup dry sherry or port
1 tablespoon sugar
5 thinly cut and seeded
    lemon slices

Optional:
1 cup roasted chestnut
    meats

SERVES 4

In a medium saucepan, cover prunes with cold water and sherry or port. Bring to a boil over medium-high heat. Reduce heat and simmer 2 minutes. Mix in sugar and lemon slices, then cook another 3 minutes.

Place in covered jar and chill at least 4 hours. Just before serving, prunes may be stuffed with chestnut meats. Serve cold or heat briefly in oven dish.

Serving: 1/4 Recipe	Calories: 180	Protein: 2 gm
Calories from Fat: 3	Total Fat: .5 gm	Dietary Fiber: 4 gm
Saturated Fat: 0 gm	Carbs: 40 gm	Sodium: 5 mg
Component of Fat: 1%	Cholesterol: 0 mg	Calcium: 35 mg

Chestnuts have relatively little fat compared to other nuts. Three ounces of roasted chestnuts contain less than 1 gram of fat, while three ounces of assorted dry roasted nuts have over 45 grams of fat!

Apple-Walnut Pancakes

SERVES 4

2 cups all-purpose flour
1 tablespoon baking powder
$1/4$ teaspoon salt
1 tablespoon sugar
2 eggs, separated
1 cup unsweetened
    applesauce
1 cup skim milk
2 tablespoons canola oil
3 tablespoons chopped
    walnuts

Sift together all dry ingredients. In a separate bowl beat egg yolks, applesauce, milk and oil. Gently mix dry and wet ingredients together.

Whip egg whites into soft peaks and gently fold into batter. Stir in chopped walnuts.

Spray hot griddle with non-stick oil. Pour one-third cup batter per pancake, cook on each side until light golden brown.

Serving: 1/4 Recipe	Calories: 411	Protein: 13 gm
Calories from Fat: 121	Total Fat: 13.5 gm	Dietary Fiber: 2 gm
Saturated Fat: 2 gm	Carbs: 60 gm	Sodium: 509 mg
Component of Fat: 29%	Cholesterol: 107 mg	Calcium: 225 mg

Apple Maple Syrup

MAKES $1^1/4$ CUPS

1 cup maple syrup
$1/4$ cup frozen apple juice
    concentrate
3-inch cinnamon stick

Put all ingredients together in saucepan and simmer on medium heat for 15 minutes. Remove cinnamon stick and serve warm.

Serving: 4 Tablespoons	Calories: 411	Protein: 13 gm
Calories from Fat: 121	Total Fat: 13.5 gm	Dietary Fiber: 2 gm
Saturated Fat: 2 gm	Carbs: 60 gm	Sodium: 509 mg
Component of Fat: 29%	Cholesterol: 107 mg	Calcium: 225 mg

Buckwheat Ployes

SERVES 4

1 cup buckwheat flour
$1/2$ cup all-purpose flour
1 teaspoon baking powder
$1/2$ teaspoon baking soda
1 teaspoon sugar
1 egg
$1^1/_4$ cups skim milk
2 tablespoons non-fat sour
     cream or plain yogurt
2 tablespoons canola oil

Sift dry ingredients into medium-sized bowl. In a separate bowl, whip wet ingredients. Combine mixtures and beat until smooth.

Spray hot griddle with non-stick oil. Ladle out 3 tablespoons batter. Using circular motion with back of spoon spread to $1/8$-inch thick. Cook $1^1/_2$ minutes on just one side.

Serving: 1/4 Recipe	Calories: 270	Protein: 10 gm
Calories from Fat: 85	Total Fat: 9.5 gm	Dietary Fiber: 3 gm
Saturated Fat: 1 gm	Carbs: 38 gm	Sodium: 325 mg
Component of Fat: 31%	Cholesterol: 54 mg	Calcium: 165 mg

Apricot Butter

SERVES 4

2 cups dried apricots
$1^1/_2$ cups apple cider
1 teaspoon lemon juice
1 teaspoon nutmeg

Chop apricots. Simmer in cider 20 minutes, stir in lemon juice and nutmeg. Purée until smooth.

Serving: 1/2 Cup	Calories: 204	Protein: 3 gm
Calories from Fat: 5	Total Fat: .5 gm	Dietary Fiber: 6 gm
Saturated Fat: 0 gm	Carbs: 53 gm	Sodium: 9 mg
Component of Fat: 2%	Cholesterol: 0 mg	Calcium: 36 mg

French-style Canadian buckwheat pancakes, called "Ployes," have long been a staple in the northern Maine woods and coastal towns. They are thin and can be rolled up with jams, syrup, spreads, caviar or smoked fish. Ployes are viewed as a bread to be served at any meal. They freeze well and can be quickly reheated in an oven before serving.

Winter Squash Waffles

SERVES 4

1 cup winter squash,
   boiled and mashed
2 eggs
1 cup skim milk
2 tablespoons canola oil
1 cup all-purpose flour
1 tablespoon double-acting
   baking powder
1 tablespoon sugar
$\frac{1}{4}$ teaspoon cinnamon
$\frac{1}{4}$ teaspoon nutmeg
2 egg whites

Mix together mashed winter squash, whole eggs, milk and oil. In a separate bowl, sift together the dry ingredients. Stir into winter squash mixture.

Beat egg whites until soft peaks form. Gently fold whites into batter. Cook in preheated waffle griddle sprayed with non-stick oil.

Serving: 1/4 Recipe	Calories: 265	Protein: 10 gm
Calories from Fat: 92	Total Fat: 10 gm	Dietary Fiber: 2 gm
Saturated Fat: 1.5 gm	Carbs: 33 gm	Sodium: 392 mg
Component of Fat: 34%	Cholesterol: 107 mg	Calcium: 228 mg

Honey-Clove Syrup

SERVES 4

1 cup honey
$\frac{1}{4}$ cup water
12 whole cloves

Put honey and water in small saucepan over medium heat. Tie cloves in cheesecloth and place in saucepan. Simmer for 15 minutes, then remove spice bag. Serve warm.

Serving: 1/4 Cup	Calories: 255	Protein: 0 gm
Calories from Fat: 0	Total Fat: 0 gm	Dietary Fiber: 0 gm
Saturated Fat: 0 gm	Carbs: 69 gm	Sodium: 4 mg
Component of Fat: 0%	Cholesterol: 0 mg	Calcium: 6 mg

Lemon Waffles

SERVES 4

1 cup all-purpose flour
2 tablespoons double-acting
    baking powder
$1/4$ cup sugar
$1/4$ teaspoon baking soda
2 eggs, separated
$1/2$ cup skim milk
$1/2$ cup club soda
3 tablespoons finely
    grated lemon rind
1 teaspoon vanilla extract
3 tablespoons canola oil

Sift together dry ingredients. In a separate bowl, whip together egg yolks and all other ingredients, except egg whites. Beat egg whites to soft peaks, gently fold into batter.

Spray preheated waffle griddle with non-stick cooking oil. Spray again before ladling out batter for each waffle.

Serving: 1/4 Recipe	Calories: 298	Protein: 7 gm
Calories from Fat: 120	Total Fat: 13.5 gm	Dietary Fiber: 1 gm
Saturated Fat: 1.5 gm	Carbs: 38 gm	Sodium: 377 mg
Component of Fat: 39%	Cholesterol: 106 mg	Calcium: 205 mg

Lemon-Lime Whipped Glaze

SERVES 4

2 cups powdered sugar
$1/4$ cup lemon juice
$1/4$ cup lime juice
2 teaspoons vanilla
2 egg whites

Combine all ingredients, except egg whites, and whip together with electric beater. In a separate bowl, beat egg whites until stiff, then gently fold into glaze. Serve as sauce over waffles.

Serving: 1/4 Cup	Calories: 257	Protein: 2 gm
Calories from Fat: 1	Total Fat: 0 gm	Dietary Fiber: 0 gm
Saturated Fat: 0 gm	Carbs: 63 gm	Sodium: 28 mg
Component of Fat: 0%	Cholesterol: 0 mg	Calcium: 4 mg

Sweet Egg Kugel

8 oz. medium uncooked
    egg noodles
$^3/_4$ cup sugar
2 tablespoons cinnamon
$^1/_2$ lb. non-fat cottage
    cheese
2 tablespoons melted
    butter
1 teaspoon vanilla extract
4 eggs
1 cup skim milk
8 oz. non-fat cream
    cheese
$1^1/_2$ cups non-fat sour
    cream

SERVES 8

Boil noodles until tender but firm to the bite. Drain. In a mixing bowl whip together $^1/_2$ cup sugar, 1 tablespoon cinnamon and remaining ingredients. Stir in noodles by hand.

Pour into casserole sprayed with non-stick oil. Mix together remaining $^1/_4$ cup sugar and 1 tablespoon cinnamon. Sprinkle over kugel.

Bake in 350° oven until browned, about 45 minutes. Serve hot.

Serving: 1/8 Recipe	Calories: 360	Protein: 19 gm
Calories from Fat: 65	Total Fat: 7 gm	Dietary Fiber: 2 gm
Saturated Fat: 3 gm	Carbs: 54 gm	Sodium: 363 mg
Component of Fat: 18%	Cholesterol: 144 mg	Calcium: 208 mg

Herbed Cheddar Omelette

$^1/_2$ teaspoon dill
$^1/_2$ teaspoon parsley
$^1/_2$ teaspoon chopped
    chives
1 large egg
1 egg white
1 teaspoon water
pinch of salt and fresh
    ground pepper
1 tablespoon grated
    low-fat Cheddar
    cheese

MAKES ONE OMELETTE
Multiply ingredients by number of omelettes.

Mix together herbs in a small bowl. Set near stove with grated cheese.

Preheat 8-10 inch, non-stick omelette pan over high heat. Whisk egg and white, water, salt and pepper together in bowl. Just before pouring eggs into pan, spray with non-stick vegetable oil. Pour eggs into middle of pan ($^1/_2$ cup at a time if using a number of eggs). Shake and swirl pan to distribute eggs evenly. Rest on heat 5 seconds to firm the bottom, while sprinkling herbs and cheese on top.

Hold pan by its handle and jerk quickly towards you while tilting far edge over burner. Continue this process and omelette will roll over on itself. When omelette forms at far end, bang on handle near pan to curl edge.

Note: Have spatula handy to assist omelette in its formative stages. An omelette should be cooked in just 20-30 seconds!

Serving: 1 Omelette	Calories: 127	Protein: 15 gm
Calories from Fat: 59	Total Fat: 6.5 gm	Dietary Fiber: 0 gm
Saturated Fat: 2 gm	Carbs: 2 gm	Sodium: 275 mg
Component of Fat: 47%	Cholesterol: 217 mg	Calcium: 180 mg

Apple Jelly Roll

2 cups all-purpose flour
2 teaspoons baking
    powder
2 teaspoons sugar
2 cups skim milk
3 large eggs
2 tablespoons canola oil
1$^1/_2$ cups peeled, cored and
    grated apples
1 teaspoon lemon juice
$^1/_2$ cup sugar
1 teaspoon cinnamon
1 tablespoon water
2 teaspoons cornstarch

Roll each jelly roll with 2
tablespoons apple sauce.
Sprinkle tops with a blend
of cinnamon and sugar.

MAKES EIGHT 8-INCH JELLY ROLLS

Sift flour before measuring. Mix flour with
baking powder and 2 teaspoons sugar. Whisk in
milk, eggs and oil. Blend until perfectly
smooth. Chill in refrigerator 30 minutes.

In a covered saucepan over medium-low heat,
simmer grated apples, lemon juice, $^1/_2$ cup sugar
and cinnamon for 10 minutes. Blend
cornstarch with water, add to apples. Cook
until thickened, then keep warm on low heat.

Preheat 8-inch pan over medium-high heat.
Spray with non-stick cooking oil and quickly
pour $^1/_3$ cup of batter in middle of pan, tilt to
cover. Bottom will be lightly brown in 30
seconds, then flip and cook 20 seconds on
second side.

Serving: 1 Jelly Roll	Calories: 258	Protein: 7 gm
Calories from Fat: 53	Total Fat: 6 gm	Dietary Fiber: 2 g
Saturated Fat: 1 gm	Carbs: 44 gm	Sodium: 156 mg
Component of Fat: 20%	Cholesterol: 81 mg	Calcium: 137 mg

Fruited Breakfast Pudding

4 cups water
2 cups couscous
1$^1/_2$ cups skim milk
1 tablespoon butter
5 tablespoons sugar
pinch of salt
1 teaspoon ground
   cinnamon
1 teaspoon vanilla
1 teaspoon lemon juice
2 eggs
2 egg whites
$^1/_2$ cup dried apricots
   or apples

SERVES 8

Preheat oven to 325°.

Boil water, then add couscous. Reduce heat to low and cover. The couscous will absorb the water in about 5 minutes.

In a mixing bowl, beat together all the other ingredients, except the dried fruit. Stir in couscous, then the dried fruit. Mix well.

Pour into baking dish sprayed with non-stick oil. If desired, sprinkle tops with additional cinnamon and sugar. Bake 45 minutes. Pudding can be served warm or cold.

Serving: 1/8 Recipe	Calories: 278	Protein: 10 gm
Calories from Fat: 29	Total Fat: 3 gm	Dietary Fiber: 3 gm
Saturated Fat: 1.5 gm	Carbs: 51 gm	Sodium: 92 mg
Component of Fat: 10%	Cholesterol: 58 mg	Calcium: 84 mg

Herbal Christmas Wreath: To a spruce, pine or fir wreath, add sprigs of dried opal basil, winter savory, cinnamon sticks, anise-hyssop, bee balm, white peppermint blossoms, hydrangea and colored sage. These herbs can also be hung in small bunches from the tree, used to make a holiday center-piece or tied with ribbon on top of pomander balls.

Cornmeal Mush

2 cups boiling skim milk
2 cups boiling water
1 cup cornmeal
$1/2$ cup cold water
pinch of salt
4 tablespoons maple syrup
    or molasses

SERVES 4

Fill bottom pan of a double boiler with water and bring to a boil. In the top pan, pour in 2 cups each boiling milk and water.

In a mixing bowl, stir together cornmeal, $1/2$ cup cold water and salt. Slowly add cornmeal mixture to hot liquids in double boiler. Stir over boiling water for 3 minutes. Reduce heat to moderate, cover and cook 30 minutes more, stirring frequently.

Serve in bowls with a tablespoon of maple syrup or molasses.

Serving: 1/4 Recipe	Calories: 202	Protein: 7 gm
Calories from Fat: 12	Total Fat: 1.5 gm	Dietary Fiber: 2 gm
Saturated Fat: .5 gm	Carbs: 42 gm	Sodium: 109 mg
Component of Fat: 6%	Cholesterol: 2 mg	Calcium: 176 mg

Maple Walnut Oatmeal

This recipe is made with whole rolled oats, not the quick variety.
The flavor and texture far surpasses processed oatmeal.

$2^3/_4$ cups water
1 cup skim milk
pinch of salt
1 cup whole rolled oats
2 tablespoons chopped
    walnuts
2 tablespoons maple syrup

SERVES 2

Boil water, milk and salt. Add rolled oats. Cook 10 minutes, stirring occasionally. Cover pot, remove from heat and let stand 5 minutes.

Serve each bowl of oatmeal with 1 tablespoon of chopped walnuts and maple syrup.

Serving: 1/2 Recipe	Calories: 454	Protein: 15 gm
Calories from Fat: 71	Total Fat: 8 gm	Dietary Fiber: 1 gm
Saturated Fat: 1 gm	Carbs: 83 gm	Sodium: 136 mg
Component of Fat: 15%	Cholesterol: 2 mg	Calcium: 215 mg

Breads
and
Baked Goods

CONTENTS

Sweet baked goods are also in the chapter "Desserts and Sweets."
Spreads for bread are located in "Appetizers and Finger Food."

Note: The nutritional analysis for breads is based on 12 slices per bread loaf.

Cranberry-Orange Muffins

1 cup chopped fresh
   or frozen cranberries
$3/4$ cup sugar
$1^3/4$ cups all-purpose flour
pinch of salt
2 teaspoons double-acting
   baking powder
1 teaspoon cinnamon
1 teaspoon ground ginger
1 egg
3 tablespoons canola oil
$1/2$ cup orange juice
$1/4$ cup skim milk
1 tablespoon finely grated
   orange rind

MAKES 12 MUFFINS

Preheat oven to 400°. Lightly spray muffin tins with non-stick oil.

Mix cranberries with sugar and set aside. Sift together flour, salt, baking powder and spices. In a separate bowl, beat together remaining ingredients. With a few swift strokes, briefly stir mixtures together and add cranberries (some lumps will remain.)

Fill muffin tins two-thirds full. Bake 20 minutes, or until a toothpick inserted in the center of muffins comes out clean.

Serving: 1 Muffin	Calories: 159	Protein: 3 gm
Calories from Fat: 36	Total Fat: 4 gm	Dietary Fiber: 1 gm
Saturated Fat: .5 gm	Carbs: 28 gm	Sodium: 100 mg
Component of Fat: 23%	Cholesterol: 18 mg	Calcium: 61 mg

Raisin-Yam Bran Muffins

A tongue-twister of a name, guaranteed easier to eat than to say.

1¹/₂ cups all-purpose flour
¹/₂ teaspoon salt
2 teaspoons baking
    powder
1 teaspoon baking soda
1 teaspoon ground cloves
1 teaspoon cinnamon
¹/₂ cup bran flakes
1¹/₄ cups packed brown
    sugar
¹/₂ cup skim milk
2 eggs
3 tablespoons canola oil
1 cup cold cooked
    mashed yams or
    sweet potatoes
¹/₂ cup raisins

MAKES 18 MUFFINS

Preheat oven to 350°. Lightly spray muffin tins with non-stick oil.

Sift together flour, salt, baking powder, baking soda and spices. Stir in bran flakes.

In a separate bowl, beat together brown sugar, milk, eggs and oil. Blend in mashed yams. Slowly add dry ingredients to yam mixture. Beat well, so batter is smooth. Fold in raisins.

Fill muffin tins two-thirds full. Bake 20-25 minutes, or until toothpick inserted in the center of muffins comes out clean.

Serving: 1 Muffin	Calories: 147	Protein: 2 gm
Calories from Fat: 29	Total Fat: 3 gm	Dietary Fiber: 1 gm
Saturated Fat: .5 gm	Carbs: 28 gm	Sodium: 218 mg
Component of Fat: 19%	Cholesterol: 24 mg	Calcium: 63 mg

Buttermilk Pineapple Muffins

2 cups sifted all-purpose
    flour
2 teaspoons double-acting
    baking powder
$1/2$ teaspoon baking soda
pinch of salt
2 tablespoons sugar
1 cup low-fat buttermilk
1 egg, beaten
$1/4$ cup skim milk
2 tablespoons canola oil
$1/2$ cup crushed pineapple,
    with liquid pressed out

MAKES 12 MUFFINS

Preheat oven to 350°. Lightly spray muffin tins with non-stick oil.

Sift together flour, baking powder, baking soda and salt.

In a separate bowl, beat together sugar, buttermilk, egg, milk and oil. Briefly stir both mixtures together, adding pineapple at the same time. Batter will be lumpy.

Spoon into muffin tins. Bake 25 minutes, or until a toothpick inserted in the center of muffins comes out clean.

Serving: 1 Muffin	Calories: 118	Protein: 11 gm
Calories from Fat: 36	Total Fat: 4 gm	Dietary Fiber: 1 gm
Saturated Fat: 1 gm	Carbs: 19 gm	Sodium: 180 mg
Component of Fat: 23%	Cholesterol: 18 mg	Calcium: 82 mg

New England Woods Potpourri: Combine 1 cup cedar tips, 1 cup sweet woodruff, 1 cup sandalwood chips, and 1 cup hawthorn or juniper berries. Mix well and scent with 4 drops green forest or pine oil.

Fluffy Biscuits

2 cups sifted all-purpose
   flour
2 teaspoons double-acting
   baking powder
$\frac{1}{2}$ teaspoon baking soda
1 teaspoon sugar
pinch of salt
2 tablespoons canola oil
1 cup cold low-fat
   buttermilk

MAKES 12 LARGE BISCUITS

Set rack in middle of oven. Preheat to 400°.
Spray cookie sheet with non-stick oil.

Mix flour, baking powder, baking soda, sugar
and salt together. Slowly add oil, and use a
butter knife to "cut" oil into flour mixture until
evenly distributed.

Stir in buttermilk. Batter should form a
somewhat sticky ball, or add just enough
buttermilk to make it hold together. Flour your
hands, divide dough, and shape into biscuits.
Place on cookie sheet and bake 12-15 minutes,
or until golden on bottom.

Serving: 1 Biscuit	Calories: 100	Protein: 10 gm
Calories from Fat: 32	Total Fat: 3.5 gm	Dietary Fiber: 1 gm
Saturated Fat: 1 gm	Carbs: 16 gm	Sodium: 172 mg
Component of Fat: 23%	Cholesterol: 0 mg	Calcium: 73 mg

Oatmeal Rolls

1 cup rolled oats (not
   quick oats)
$^1/_2$ tablespoon canola oil
$^1/_2$ teaspoon salt
$1^1/_2$ cups boiling water
1 tablespoon very hot
   water
1 pkg. active dry yeast
$^1/_2$ cup molasses or honey
4 cups sifted all-purpose
   flour

MAKES 24 ROLLS

Boil water in bottom pan of a double boiler. In the top pan, combine oats, oil, salt and $1^1/_2$ cups boiling water. Cook for 30 minutes, stirring occasionally. Cool until lukewarm.

In a small cup, blend the tablespoon of very hot water with yeast. Stir yeast mixture into cooked oats. Add molasses or honey and flour. Knead until well blended. Cover, and let rise until double in bulk, about 2 hours.

Spray muffin tins with non-stick oil. With oiled hands, pinch off pieces of dough and place in tins. Let rise again until double in bulk. Bake in 400° oven for 20 minutes.

Serving: 1 Roll	Calories: 121	Protein: 3 gm
Calories from Fat: 7	Total Fat: .5 gm	Dietary Fiber: 1 gm
Saturated Fat: 0 gm	Carbs: 26 gm	Sodium: 50 mg
Component of Fat: 5%	Cholesterol: 0 mg	Calcium: 7 mg

Pretzels

1 cup 105°-115° water
1 pkg. active dry yeast
2³/₄ cups all-purpose
    flour
2 tablespoons soft butter
¹/₂ teaspoon salt
1 tablespoon sugar
4 cups water
5 teaspoons baking soda

Optional:
coarse salt or sea salt

MAKES TWELVE 6-INCH PRETZELS

Combine 1 cup warm water and yeast. Let set 5 minutes, stir until dissolved. Add 1¹/₂ cups of the flour, butter, salt and sugar. Beat at least 3 minutes. Stir in remaining 1¹/₄ cup flour and knead until dough is no longer sticky.

Cover, and let rise in bowl until double in bulk. Punch down and divide into 12 equal pieces. Roll pieces between palms into 18-inch pencil-thin lengths. Spray cookie sheet with non-stick oil. Loop into twisted oval pretzel shape. Place on cookie sheet and let rise until double in bulk.

Boil water with baking soda in a non-aluminum pot. One at a time, gently remove pretzels with slotted spatula and lower into boiling water for 1 minute or until they float. Return to cookie sheet, sprinkle with salt, if desired. Bake in 475° oven 10-12 minutes.

Serving: 1 Pretzel	Calories: 120	Protein: 3 gm
Calories from Fat: 21	Total Fat: 2.5 gm	Dietary Fiber: 1 gm
Saturated Fat: 1.5 gm	Carbs: 22 gm	Sodium: 124 mg
Component of Fat: 17%	Cholesterol: 5 mg	Calcium: 6 mg

French Onion Sticks

3¹/₄ cups flour
1 tablespoon sugar
pinch of salt
1 pkg. active dry yeast
1 cup warm water
6 tablespoons olive oil
1 cup grated onion

MAKES 24 STICKS

Combine 1 cup of the flour with sugar, salt and yeast. Add water, beating until smooth. Mix in 3 tablespoons of the olive oil and 1¹/₄-cups more flour. Beat well. Turn onto board, knead in remaining flour. Continue kneading until smooth (add flour if dough is sticky).

Place in bowl sprayed with non-stick oil, turning to coat all sides. Cover, let rise until doubled in bulk. Punch down.

Saute onions in 2 tablespoons olive oil. Knead onions into dough, then divide into 24 balls. Roll balls between palms to form 8-inch sticks. Place on cookie sheet sprayed with non-stick oil. Brush sticks with olive oil. Let rise until double in bulk. Bake in 400° oven 12-15 minutes.

Serving: 1 Stick	Calories: 92	Protein: 2 gm
Calories from Fat: 32	Total Fat: 3.5 gm	Dietary Fiber: 1 gm
Saturated Fat: .5 gm	Carbs: 13 gm	Sodium: 6 mg
Component of Fat: 35%	Cholesterol: 0 mg	Calcium: 4 mg

COASTAL NEW ENGLAND   WINTERFARE COOKING

Egg Challah

This easy bread is healthy and beautiful.
Serve whole and warm, inviting everyone to twist off a piece of the braid.

2 pkgs. active dry yeast
1 teaspoon sugar
$\frac{1}{4}$ cup very warm water
6 cups all-purpose flour
1 teaspoon salt
2 cups very warm water
3 eggs, slightly beaten
3 tablespoons canola oil
3 tablespoons sugar
2 cups flour for kneading
1 egg yolk
2 tablespoons skim milk
4 tablespoons poppy seeds

MAKES 2 LOAVES

With a small whisk, beat yeast, 1 teaspoon sugar and $\frac{1}{4}$ cup very warm water. In large bowl combine 6 cups flour and salt. Make a deep well in center of the flour, pour in yeast mixture. Add warm water, eggs, oil and remaining sugar. Beat well, then turn onto floured board. Knead until dough is smooth and elastic. Place in bowl sprayed with vegetable oil, turning to coat all sides. Cover, and let rise until double in bulk. Punch down, knead briefly, then divide in half.

Cut each half into 3 sections. Roll sections into 18-inch long tapered ropes. Place the 3 ropes side-by-side on a cookie sheet (sprayed with non-stick oil). Starting in the middle, braid ropes to both ends and tuck ends under. Cover, and let rise until doubled in bulk. Brush tops with egg yolk beaten with skim milk, sprinkle with poppy seeds. Bake at 400° 15 minutes, reduce to 375° and bake 20 minutes more.

Serving: 1 Slice
Calories from Fat: 32
Saturated Fat: .5 gm
Component of Fat: 18%

Calories: 183
Total Fat: 3.5 gm
Carbs: 32 gm
Cholesterol: 35 mg

Protein: 5 gm
Dietary Fiber: 1 gm
Sodium: 108 mg
Calcium: 33 mg

Low-Fat Basic Bread

1 cup warm water
2 tablespoons sugar
1 pkg. active dry yeast
$1/_2$ teaspoon sea salt
2 tablespoons safflower
  oil
2 tablespoons sesame
  seeds
3 cups unbleached flour

Kneading:
1-2 cups flour

Loaf Crusts:
3 tablespoons sesame
  seeds
1 tablespoon skim milk

MAKES 2 LOAVES

In a large bowl, combine water, sugar and yeast. Let rest 5 minutes, then stir. Mix in remaining ingredients in order listed. Knead about 10 minutes, working in additional flour. Spray a bowl with vegetable oil. Place dough in bowl, turn to coat all sides. Cover, and let rise until doubled in bulk.

Spray two 9" x 5" bread pans with non-stick oil. Dust each pan with a tablespoon of sesame seeds. Punch down dough and shape into two 9-inch loaves. Place in pans. Brush milk over the tops and sprinkle with remaining sesame seeds. Cover, let rise until double in bulk. Bake in 400° oven 30 minutes.

Serving: 1 Slice	Calories: 105	Protein: 3 gm
Calories from Fat: 20	Total Fat: 2.5 gm	Dietary Fiber: 1 gm
Saturated Fat: .5 gm	Carbs: 18 gm	Sodium: 50 mg
Component of Fat: 20%	Cholesterol: 0 mg	Calcium: 23 mg

Safflower oil, a healthy oil very low in saturated fat, was considered the least desirable of oils in Old World cooking. Even in India, only the poorest people benefited by using safflower oil. Historically, the healthier, natural food products have been left for the poor, as in China where only the humblest citizens once ate whole grain brown rice.

Swedish Buttermilk Rye Bread

$^1/_2$ cup very warm water
2 pkgs. active dry yeast
1 cup low-fat buttermilk
$^1/_2$ cup molasses
3 tablespoons canola oil
1 teaspoon salt
2 tablespoons finely
    grated orange rind
2 tablespoons caraway
    seeds
$2^1/_2$ cups finely milled rye
    flour, sifted
3 cups all-purpose flour,
    plus 1 cup flour for
    kneading
1 tablespoon skim milk
2 teaspoons caraway
    seeds

MAKES 2 LOAVES

In a large bowl, dissolve yeast in water. In a small saucepan, warm buttermilk, molasses and oil, then add to yeast mixture. Mix in salt, grated rind and 2 tablespoons caraway seeds. Stir in flours. Turn out and knead 10 minutes on floured board. Spray another bowl with vegetable oil. Place dough in bowl, turning to coat all sides. Cover, and let rise until double in bulk.

Spray two 9" x 5" bread pans with non-stick oil. Punch down dough, and shape into two 9-inch loaves. Place in pans. With a very sharp knife, make four $^1/_4$-inch deep diagonal slashes in the tops of the loaves. Brush milk over the tops and sprinkle with remaining caraway seeds. Cover, let rise until double in bulk. Bake in 375° oven 35 minutes.

Serving: 1 Slice	Calories: 150	Protein: 8 gm
Calories from Fat: 25	Total Fat: 2.5 gm	Dietary Fiber: 2 gm
Saturated Fat: .5 gm	Carbs: 29 gm	Sodium: 115 mg
Component of Fat: 14%	Cholesterol: 0 mg	Calcium: 38 mg

Potato Bread

$^3/_4$ cup very warm water
1 teaspoon sugar
2 pkgs. active dry yeast
$1^1/_2$ cup mashed potatoes
$1^1/_2$ cups low-fat
    buttermilk
4 tablespoons melted
    butter
$^1/_2$ cup honey
2 teaspoons salt
2 cups oat, rice or whole
    wheat flour
$^1/_3$ cup wheat germ
$4^1/_2$ cups all-purpose flour

MAKES 3 LOAVES

Dissolve the yeast and sugar in water. In a large bowl, mix mashed potatoes, buttermilk, butter, honey and salt. Beat for 2 minutes, then add yeast mixture. Stir in oat, rice or wheat flour, wheat germ and 2 cups all-purpose flour. Turn onto floured board and work in remaining flour. Knead 8 minutes, adding flour as needed to keep dough from sticking.

Place in bowl sprayed with non-stick oil, turning dough to coat all sides. Cover, and let rise until double in bulk. Punch down, then shape into 3 loaves. Place each loaf in a 9" x 5" bread pan that's been sprayed with non-stick oil. Let rise until double in bulk. Bake in 375° oven 35 minutes.

Serving: 1 Slice	Calories: 121	Protein: 7 gm
Calories from Fat: 23	Total Fat: 2.5 gm	Dietary Fiber: 2 gm
Saturated Fat: 1.5 gm	Carbs: 22 gm	Sodium: 174 mg
Component of Fat: 16%	Cholesterol: 4 mg	Calcium: 21 mg

Sourdough Brown Bread

Sourdough Starter:
1 pkg. active dry yeast
2 cups lukewarm water
2 cups all-purpose flour
1 tablespoon dark
    molasses

Sourdough:
1 cup sourdough starter
$^{1}/_{2}$ cup low-fat buttermilk
1 cup dark molasses
2 tablespoons sugar
$^{1}/_{2}$ teaspoon salt
2 cups graham flour
2 cups sifted all-purpose
    flour

MAKES 9" x 5" LOAF

Sourdough Starter: Combine all ingredients in a wide-mouthed crockery or glass jar. Stir with a wooden spoon (never metal.) Leave uncovered at 80° for 4-7 days. Stir down each day and whenever a crust forms. Starter is ready for use, or storage in the refrigerator, when it bubbles and emits a sour odor.

In a large mixing bowl, stir sourdough ingredients, one at a time, into sourdough starter in the order they are listed.

Spray a 9" x 5" bread pan with non-stick oil. Pour batter into pan and let rise until double in bulk. Bake in 350° oven 1 hour or until bread sounds hollow when tapped.

Serving: 1 Slice	Calories: 297	Protein: 11 gm
Calories from Fat: 12	Total Fat: 1.5 gm	Dietary Fiber: 4 gm
Saturated Fat: .5 gm	Carbs: 66 gm	Sodium: 125 mg
Component of Fat: 4%	Cholesterol: 0 mg	Calcium: 85 mg

Quick Pumpkin-Orange Bread

1 cup cooked or canned
    mashed pumpkin
1 cup sugar
$^1/_2$ cup brown sugar
$^1/_4$ cup canola oil
1 egg
1 egg white
$^1/_2$ cup orange juice
1 teaspoon vanilla extract
$1^3/_4$ cups all-purpose flour
2 teaspoons baking powder
$^1/_2$ teaspoon baking soda
$^1/_2$ teaspoon cinnamon
$^1/_2$ teaspoon ground cloves

Optional:
$^1/_2$ cup chopped dates

MAKES ONE 9" x 5" LOAF

Preheat oven to 350°. Beat together mashed pumpkin, sugars, oil, eggs, orange juice and vanilla. Sift together dry ingredients. Very briefly stir the dry mixture into the pumpkin blend, with just a few strokes. Quickly stir in chopped dates, if desired.

Spray a 9" x 5" bread pan, or two mini pans, with non-stick oil. Pour batter into pan, bake 50 minutes (less for mini-pans). Remove from oven when toothpick inserted in center of bread comes out clean. Leave in pan 10 minutes before turning onto wire rack to cool.

Serving: 1 Slice	Calories: 219	Protein: 3 gm
Calories from Fat: 46	Total Fat: 5 gm	Dietary Fiber: 1 gm
Saturated Fat: .5 gm	Carbs: 41 gm	Sodium: 148 mg
Component of Fat: 21%	Cholesterol: 18 mg	Calcium: 64 mg

Hot Cross Buns

1 cup skim milk
$^3/_4$ cup sugar
$^1/_2$ teaspoon cinnamon
1 tablespoon finely grated
   orange rind
$^1/_2$ cup currants or raisins
2 tablespoons butter
$^1/_4$ teaspoon salt
1 pkg. active dry yeast
2 tablespoons hot water
1 egg
2$^2/_3$ cup all-purpose flour

Milk Glaze:
$^3/_4$ cup powdered sugar,
   sifted
2 tablespoons hot skim
   milk
$^1/_2$ teaspoon vanilla

MAKES 18 BUNS

Scald milk. Remove from heat. Add sugar, cinnamon, grated orange rind, currants or raisins, butter and salt.

In a separate bowl, sprinkle yeast over hot (not boiling) water. Rest 5 minutes, then stir milk mixture into yeast mixture. Beat in egg. Mix in most of the flour, then knead in the rest. Place in bowl, cover with floured towel, and let rise until double in bulk.

Preheat oven to 400°. Spray large cake pan with non-stick vegetable oil. Punch down dough and roll into 18 balls. Place in prepared pan and press down to flatten buns. Cover, and let rise until double in bulk. Bake at 400° for 20 minutes, or until light golden. Mix powdered sugar with hot milk and vanilla. Drizzle over buns in classic cross pattern, or swirl over tops.

Serving: 1 Bun	Calories: 147	Protein: 3 gm
Calories from Fat: 17	Total Fat: 2 gm	Dietary Fiber: 1 gm
Saturated Fat: 1 gm	Carbs: 30 gm	Sodium: 59 mg
Component of Fat: 11%	Cholesterol: 16 mg	Calcium: 27 mg

Appetizers
and
Finger Food

CONTENTS

Appetizers can be used as a main dish by
doubling the amount of food per serving.

Shrimp and Lobster Remoulade

1¹/₂ lbs. cooked shrimp,
    peeled and deveined
2 cups cooked lobster meat,
    cut in small pieces
1 cup non-fat mayonnaise
¹/₃ cup low-sodium chili
    sauce
1 teaspoon grated onion
1 tablespoon parsley
2 teaspoons Worcestershire
    sauce
1 teaspoon horseradish
2 teaspoons sweet pickle
    relish
1 teaspoon Dijon mustard
1 tablespoon capers,
    rinsed and drained

SERVES 10

Toss shrimp and lobster meat together. Chill.

In a large mixing bowl, blend all remaining ingredients. Gently fold in shrimp and lobster. Place in a serving bowl. Cover with plastic wrap and refrigerate at least a few hours, but preferably overnight.

Serve with cocktail forks or on appetizer plates. Your guests will love you for this!

Serving: 1/10 Recipe	Calories: 124	Protein: 20 gm
Calories from Fat: 9	Total Fat: 1 gm	Dietary Fiber: 0 gm
Saturated Fat: .5 gm	Carbs: 6 gm	Sodium: 490 mg
Component of Fat: 8%	Cholesterol: 154 mg	Calcium: 49 mg

View from Cadillac Mountain
Mount Desert Island, Maine

Oysters Rockefeller

SERVES 6

24 medium-sized oysters
  on the half shell
rock salt to set oysters on
2 bags spinach, cooked
  and well drained
1/4 cup grated onion
2 tablespoons olive oil
1 tablespoon soft butter
1/2 cup dry bread crumbs
1 tablespoon parsley
6 drops hot pepper sauce

Optional:
2 teaspoons anisette

Preheat oven to 475°. Pour rock salt in baking dishes, at least 1 inch thick. Embed oysters in the rock salt, sunny-side up, to balance and protect them from overcooking.

Press moisture out of spinach, so it is quite dry. Chop very fine. Sauté onion in olive oil.

Mix spinach, onion and butter in bowl, then add remaining ingredients. Spread mixture on oysters. Bake in oven 10 minutes or until plump, then broil until browned. Serve hot.

Serving: 4 Oysters	Calories: 158	Protein: 10 gm
Calories from Fat: 70	Total Fat: 8 gm	Dietary Fiber: 4 gm
Saturated Fat: 2.5 gm	Carbs: 15 gm	Sodium: 337 mg
Component of Fat: 42%	Cholesterol: 35 mg	Calcium: 199 mg

Artifacts recently found at Bull Brook in Ipswich, Massachusetts, suggest that the first people came to the New England coastal region around 8,000 B.C. Their ancestors had crossed the land bridge over the Bering Sea 20,000 years ago, and their decendents left enormous oyster piles on the banks of the Damariscotta and Kennebec Rivers in Maine.

Asparagus Cheese Puffs

SERVES 4

1 cup cooked asparagus,
    fresh, frozen or canned
2 egg whites
2 tablespoons softened
    low-fat cream cheese
3 tablespoons grated
    Parmesan cheese
3 tablespoons non-fat
    mayonnaise
1 teaspoon paprika
pinch of curry
pinch of salt
pinch of pepper
24 crackers or Melba toast
    rounds

Preheat broiler. Cut asparagus into small pieces and coarsely mash.

Beat egg whites until stiff. In a separate bowl, blend together cream cheese, Parmesan, mayonnaise and spices. Fold egg whites into cheese mixture. Gently add asparagus. Heap onto crackers or Melba toast rounds, then place on cookie sheet. Watch closely under broiler, remove when puffs are light gold. Serve hot.

Serving: 6 Crackers
Calories from Fat: 33
Saturated Fat: 2 gm
Component of Fat: 18%

Calories: 180
Total Fat: 3.5 gm
Carbs: 28 gm
Cholesterol: 7 mg

Protein: 9 gm
Dietary Fiber: 3 gm
Sodium: 250 mg
Calcium: 102 mg

Vegetable Spring Rolls

Like all of America's immigrants, those recently arriving from Asia have enhanced the local cuisine. These spring rolls use local winter vegetables.

$1/2$ cup cider vinegar

6 tablespoons sugar

pinch of cayenne

$1/2$ teaspoon salt

1 garlic clove, minced

2 cups fresh bean sprouts

2 cups shredded Chinese
    cabbage

1 cup thinly sliced carrots

1 tablespoon grated onion

$1/2$ cup slivered water
    chestnuts

1 tablespoon cornstarch

8 spring-roll or egg-roll
    wrappers

$1/4$ cup canola oil for frying

SERVES 8

Whisk vinegar and sugar together in a large mixing bowl. Stir in spices, garlic, sprouts, cabbage, carrots, onion and water chestnuts. Let sit for one hour, then drain in a colander. Return to bowl, mix in cornstarch.

Fill and roll up spring-roll or egg-roll wrappers according to manufacturer's instructions. Pour 2 tablespoons of oil into frying pan and set on medium-high heat. It will take about 7 minutes before oil is hot enough. Carefully place rolls in pan, turning until brown on all sides (about 5-6 minutes). Drain on paper towels.

Serving: 1 Spring Roll	Calories: 140	Protein: 3 gm
Calories from Fat: 49	Total Fat: 5.5 gm	Dietary Fiber: 2 gm
Saturated Fat: .5 gm	Carbs: 22 gm	Sodium: 208 mg
Component of Fat: 33%	Cholesterol: 1 mg	Calcium: 40 mg

Crab Toasts

1 lb. crab meat, well
    drained
pinch of salt
1 tablespoon sherry
1 scallion, chopped fine
1 egg, beaten
3 tablespoons almond
    slivers
$1/2$ teaspoon ginger
2 teaspoons cornstarch
6 slices white bread
2 tablespoons canola oil
    for frying

MAKES 2 DOZEN

Mix together crab meat, salt, sherry, scallion, egg, almond slivers, ginger and cornstarch. Let mixture rest 15 minutes.

Spray a large frying pan with non-stick oil. Pour $1/4$ inch canola oil into pan and preheat on medium-high.

Trim crust from bread slices, then cut each piece into four triangles. Spread each triangle with 1 tablespoon crab mixture. Spray frying pan with non-stick oil, then coat with canola oil. Fry, crab side down, until golden brown. Remove with slotted spatula and drain on paper towels.

Serving: 2 Toasts	Calories: 104	Protein: 9 gm
Calories from Fat: 45	Total Fat: 5 gm	Dietary Fiber: 1 gm
Saturated Fat: .5 gm	Carbs: 7 gm	Sodium: 264 mg
Component of Fat: 42%	Cholesterol: 55 mg	Calcium: 38 mg

COASTAL NEW ENGLAND WINTERFARE COOKING

Marinated Shrimp
with Artichoke Hearts

1$\frac{1}{2}$ lbs. large shrimp,
  cooked, peeled and
  deveined
8-oz. can artichoke hearts
12 mushrooms
1 sweet onion, Vidalia or
  purple
8 pitted black olives
3$\frac{1}{2}$-oz. jar drained and
  rinsed capers
1 pint cherry tomatoes

Marinade:
1 cup safflower oil
$\frac{3}{4}$ cup cider vinegar
3 tablespoons
  Worcestershire sauce
2 teaspoons Tabasco
1 tablespoon sugar
$\frac{1}{2}$ teaspoon pepper

SERVES 8

Place shrimp in a wide shallow container. Chop artichoke hearts into bite-sized pieces; mushrooms in half to show shape; onion into thin rings; and olives into round halves. Mix vegetables with capers, tomatoes and shrimp.

In a separate bowl, mix marinade ingredients. Pour over shrimp and vegetables. Cover container and chill at least 24 hours, stirring occasionally. Drain off marinade before serving.

Serving: 1/8 Recipe
Calories from Fat: 41
Saturated Fat: .5 gm
Component of Fat: 28%

Calories: 146
Total Fat: 4.5 gm
Carbs: 7 gm
Cholesterol: 166 mg

Protein: 19 gm
Dietary Fiber: 1 gm
Sodium: 413 mg
Calcium: 40 mg

Pickled Oysters or Mussels

2 quarts oysters or mussels
1 quart oyster liquor, clam
    juice or fish broth
1 tablespoon peppercorns
1 tablespoon allspice
1 thinly sliced lemon
1 tablespoon vinegar
1 teaspoon minced garlic

SERVES 4

Thoroughly scrub oysters or mussels, discarding any that do not close. In a large pot, cook oysters or mussels in the liquid until shells open (about 15 minutes). Strain liquid through a fine sieve and reserve. Remove meat from shells.

Combine shucked oysters or mussels with strained liquid and remaining ingredients. Place in large container and cover. Let cool to room temperature, then chill for at least 24 hours before serving.

Serving: 1/4 Recipe	Calories: 155	Protein: 16 gm
Calories from Fat: 50	Total Fat: 5.5 gm	Dietary Fiber: 0 gm
Saturated Fat: 1.5 gm	Carbs: 9 gm	Sodium: 514 mg
Component of Fat: 33%	Cholesterol: 119 mg	Calcium: 102 mg

In 1853, Mrs. J. Chadwick of Boston wrote *Home Cookery*, prescribing the addition of oysters in everything from bean soup to gumbo. Oyster wagons from Chesapeake Bay rolled through the streets of Boston and other New England towns. "Oyster Houses" in coastal cities offered oysters stewed, spiced, fried, baked, grilled, pickled and fricasseed.

Clam Balls

SERVES 6

1¹/₂ cups chopped clams,
    well drained
6 medium potatoes,
    baked and scooped
    out of the skin
2 eggs
2 tablespoons low-fat
    buttermilk
2 teaspoons grated onions
1 teaspoon Dijon mustard
1 teaspoon tarragon
salt and pepper to taste
skim milk for dipping
flour for dipping
3 tablespoons canola oil for
    frying

Wash clam meat. Rice or mash potatoes, then mix with chopped clams. One at a time, beat in eggs, then blend in buttermilk, onions and spices. Roll into 1-inch balls. Spray frying pan with non-stick oil. Pour in canola oil, heat on medium-high 7 minutes.

Dip clam balls in milk, then roll in flour. Fry until light brown. Serve with toothpicks and Tartar Sauce.

Serving: 1/6 Recipe	Calories: 297	Protein: 18 gm
Calories from Fat: 73	Total Fat: 8 gm	Dietary Fiber: 3 gm
Saturated Fat: 1 gm	Carbs: 40 gm	Sodium: 106 mg
Component of Fat: 24%	Cholesterol: 98 mg	Calcium: 66 mg

Classic Tartar Sauce

MAKES 1¹/₄ CUPS

1 cup non-fat mayonnaise, 1 teaspoon mustard, 1 tablespoon parsley, 1 tablespoon pickle relish, 2 teaspoons lemon juice, 1 teaspoon grated shallots, 1 tablespoon chopped capers, salt and pepper to taste.

Serving: 1 Tablespoon   Calories: 10   Protein: 0 gm   Calories from Fat: 0   Total Fat: 0 gm   Dietary Fiber: 0 gm
Saturated Fat: 0 gm Carbs: 2 gm   Sodium: 113 mg   Component of Fat: 2%   Cholesterol: 0 mg   Calcium: 1 mg

Black-Eyed Pea Caviar

16 oz. can black-eyed peas,
   drained
16 oz. can white hominy,
   drained
2 medium tomatoes
4 green onions
1 large clove garlic
1 pepper, any color
$\frac{1}{4}$ cup chopped cilantro
2 tablespoons parsley
$\frac{1}{2}$ cup picante sauce
   (mild, medium or hot)

Serving Suggestions:
baked tortilla chips
crackers
vegetable dippers

SERVES 10

Combine black-eyed peas and hominy in a mixing bowl. Slice tomatoes in half, remove seeds, then chop into small pieces. Using just the white and green tender bases of the green onion, slice into small thin slivers. Crush garlic clove. Dice pepper. Combine all ingredients with black-eyed peas and hominy. Mix well and serve cold.

Serving: 1/4 Cup	Calories: 61	Protein: 2 gm
Calories from Fat: 6	Total Fat: .5 gm	Dietary Fiber: 3 gm
Saturated Fat: 0 gm	Carbs: 12 gm	Sodium: 181 mg
Component of Fat: 9%	Cholesterol: 0 mg	Calcium: 18 mg

COASTAL NEW ENGLAND   WINTERFARE COOKING

Baked-Stuffed Mushroom Caps

1 lb. large cap mushrooms
1 cup plain bread crumbs
1 teaspoon rosemary,
    oregano or basil
pinch of pepper
pinch of salt
1 tablespoon safflower oil
2 tablespoons wine
1 clove crushed garlic
2 tablespoons chopped
    scallions
1 teaspoon paprika for
    tops

SERVES 4

Preheat oven to 350°. Spray large baking dish with non-stick oil.

Gently pop stems out of mushroom caps. Chop stems into small pieces, combine with bread crumbs and spices. Mix well.

Heat oil and wine in a small pan, add garlic and scallion. Sauté 2 minutes, then pour into stuffing mixture. Use a fork to distribute moisture. With a small teaspoon, press stuffing into mushroom caps. Place in baking pan, sprinkle tops with paprika. Bake 15 minutes, or until lightly browned on top.

Serving: 1/4 Recipe	Calories: 175	Protein: 6 gm
Calories from Fat: 49	Total Fat: 5.5 gm	Dietary Fiber: 2 gm
Saturated Fat: .5 gm	Carbs: 26 gm	Sodium: 268 mg
Component of Fat: 27%	Cholesterol: 0 mg	Calcium: 76 mg

The native tribes who inhabited the New England region used wild mushrooms, fungi, berries, flowers and plants for medicine and cooking. These included blue and yellow flag iris, truffles, purple loosestrife, turtlehead, American ginger, May apple, snakeroot, white yarrow, alfalfa, blackberries, Indian tobacco and tansy.

Peppy Pimento Cutter Sandwiches

4 oz. non-fat cream cheese
4 oz. jar diced pimentos
8 drops Tabasco sauce
$1/2$ teaspoon lime juice
pinch of garlic powder
pinch of pepper
8 slices white bread

SERVES 4

Allow cream cheese to soften at room temperature, then place in small mixing bowl. Drain diced pimentos and add to cream cheese with Tabasco sauce, lime juice and spices. Using a fork, blend well. Adjust seasonings to taste.

Trim crust from bread. With a rolling pin, lightly roll bread slices, compacting to half their original thickness. Spread pimento mixture on a slice, and cover with another slice of rolled bread. Cut each sandwich into 4 small squares.

Serving: 1 Sandwich	Calories: 130	Protein: 8 gm
Calories from Fat: 14	Total Fat: 1.5 gm	Dietary Fiber: 4 gm
Saturated Fat: .5 gm	Carbs: 23 gm	Sodium: 424 mg
Component of Fat: 10%	Cholesterol: 2 mg	Calcium: 103 mg

Rose Salmon Dip

1 lb. fresh salmon fillet
$\frac{1}{3}$ cup non-fat cottage
    cheese
3 canned artichoke hearts
1 scallion, chopped
4 drops Tabasco sauce
1 teaspoon Dijon mustard
1 tablespoon lemon juice
1 teaspoon dill
3 tablespoons pimento

MAKES $1\frac{1}{2}$ CUPS

Poach salmon fillet in boiling water for 12 minutes. Cut salmon into pieces, and place in blender or food processor with remaining ingredients. Process until smooth. Chill. Serve with French bread, bagels, or crackers.

Serving: 1/4 Cup
Calories from Fat: 44
Saturated Fat: .5 gm
Component of Fat: 36%

Calories: 125
Total Fat: 5 gm
Carbs: 2 gm
Cholesterol: 42 mg

Protein: 17 gm
Dietary Fiber: 0 gm
Sodium: 133 mg
Calcium: 20 mg

Wickford Cove
Wickford, Rhode Island

Zesty Spinach Dip

1 lb. frozen chopped
    spinach
1 cup non-fat plain yogurt
1 cup non-fat cottage
    cheese
2 teaspoons lemon juice
6 drops Tabasco sauce
2 cloves minced garlic
2 tablespoons dill
1 teaspoon black pepper
$\frac{1}{4}$ teaspoon salt

MAKES 2$\frac{1}{2}$ CUPS

In a fine sieve, defrost, drain and press moisture from chopped spinach.

Combine yogurt and cottage cheese in a blender. Process until smooth. Add lemon juice, Tabasco, garlic and spices. Process in blender again. Pour into bowl and mix in spinach. Cover and chill in refrigerator. Serve with crackers or fresh vegetable sticks.

Serving: 1/4 Cup
Calories from Fat: 1
Saturated Fat: 0 gm
Component of Fat: 1%

Calories: 42
Total Fat: 0 gm
Carbs: 4 gm
Cholesterol: 0 mg

Protein: 5 gm
Dietary Fiber: 1 gm
Sodium: 213 mg
Calcium: 93 mg

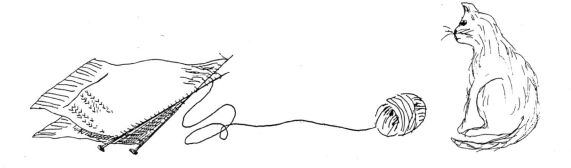

COASTAL NEW ENGLAND   WINTERFARE COOKING

Bill's Elegant Artichoke Dip

Serve with plain or cheese rice crackers
for an exquisite sensory experience.

SERVES 4

14 oz. can artichoke
    hearts in water
4 oz. non-fat cream cheese,
    softened at room
    temperature
$\frac{1}{3}$ cup low-fat mayonnaise
$\frac{1}{3}$ cup grated low-sodium
    Parmesan cheese

Preheat oven to 350°. Spray small baking dish with non-stick oil.

Drain artichokes, press out moisture, and chop into small pieces. In a mixing bowl, blend together cream cheese, mayonnaise and Parmesan. Mix in artichoke hearts. Bake 25 minutes in prepared dish. Serve hot.

Serving: 1/4 Recipe	Calories: 121	Protein: 9 gm
Calories from Fat: 42	Total Fat: 4.5 gm	Dietary Fiber: 0 gm
Saturated Fat: 2 gm	Carbs: 10 gm	Sodium: 446 mg
Component of Fat: 36%	Cholesterol: 10 mg	Calcium: 190 mg

Salads
and
Fresh Greens

COASTAL NEW ENGLAND   WINTERFARE COOKING

CONTENTS

Hot Slaw with Sunflower Seeds

*If you've been drying out last season's sunflowers
the seeds should be ready to use in this fresh hot slaw.*

SERVES 4

1/4 cup hulled sunflower
   seeds
1 egg
2 tablespoons sugar
2 tablespoons vinegar
1/2 cup apple cider
1 teaspoon tamari or
   soy sauce
pinch of pepper
4 cups grated green
   cabbage

Lightly toast sunflower seeds on ungreased cookie sheet in 350° oven.

In a large saucepan, whisk together egg, sugar, vinegar, apple cider, tamari or soy sauce and pepper. Stirring constantly, cook over medium-low heat until thickened. Stir in cabbage, cover pan. Cook just until cabbage is hot and beginning to wilt. Place in serving bowl and sprinkle with toasted sunflower seeds. Serve hot.

Serving: 1/4 Recipe	Calories: 129	Protein: 5 gm
Calories from Fat: 53	Total Fat: 6 gm	Dietary Fiber: 3 gm
Saturated Fat: 1 gm	Carbs: 17 gm	Sodium: 113 mg
Component of Fat: 38%	Cholesterol: 53 mg	Calcium: 52 mg

Sweet & Sour Kidney Bean Salad

2 cups dried kidney beans
4 tablespoons ketchup
3 tablespoons orange juice
2$\frac{1}{2}$ tablespoons olive oil
2 tablespoons vinegar
2 teaspoons lemon juice
1 tablespoon dry mustard
3 tablespoons brown
    sugar
1 teaspoon crushed garlic
2 tablespoons finely
    chopped sweet onions
    (Vidalia, red, purple)
1 teaspoon black pepper
2 tablespoons fresh
    parsley

SERVES 8

Soak kidney beans overnight. In the morning, rinse in cold water. Add beans to large pot of boiling water, cover and simmer according to package directions until tender. Drain and chill.

Combine remaining ingredients together. Mix into chilled beans. Serve cold.

Serving: 1/8 Recipe	Calories: 231	Protein: 11 gm
Calories from Fat: 44	Total Fat: 5 gm	Dietary Fiber: 12 gm
Saturated Fat: .5 gm	Carbs: 36 gm	Sodium: 82 mg
Component of Fat: 19%	Cholesterol: 0 mg	Calcium: 80 mg

The broad harbors and protected bays of coastal New England helped the Yankees to establish a maritime economy. Tall timber forests provided lumber for shipbuilding and tall masts. The first vessel was launched into the Kennebec River in 1607, the 30-ton pinnace, *Virginia*. By 1700, shipbuilding had become a major industry.

Eggplant Salad

A surprisingly good way to serve eggplant.

SERVES 5

1 large eggplant
2 tomatoes
1 red pepper, chopped
   fine
1 small onion, grated
1 clove garlic, minced
1 teaspoon savory
pinch of salt
pinch of black pepper
3 tablespoons wine
   vinegar
2 tablespoons olive oil
1 tablespoon parsley

Preheat broiler. Place eggplant on middle rack of oven, and turn it often to broil evenly on all sides. When the skin is blackened, remove eggplant and cool. Rub the skin off with a damp paper towel, and discard. Chop eggplant into small pieces.

Chop tomatoes into fine pieces, discarding excess seeds. Combine tomato with eggplant, pepper, onion and garlic.

In a small bowl, mix remaining ingredients. Pour over eggplant, toss and chill.

Serving: 1/5 Recipe	Calories: 105	Protein: 2 gm
Calories from Fat: 53	Total Fat: 6 gm	Dietary Fiber: 5 gm
Saturated Fat: 1 gm	Carbs: 13 gm	Sodium: 33 mg
Component of Fat: 46%	Cholesterol: 0 mg	Calcium: 25 mg

Veggie Medley Pasta Salad

2 lbs. fresh, refrigerated
  fettucine
1 green pepper
1 red pepper
1 head cauliflower
3 medium-sized carrots
4 radishes
12 mushrooms
1 small Vidalia, red or
  purple onion
$\frac{1}{2}$ cup wine vinegar
$\frac{1}{2}$ cup white wine
$\frac{1}{4}$ cup safflower oil
1 tablespoon sugar
2 teaspoons oregano
2 teaspoons basil
1 teaspoon tarragon
salt and pepper to taste

SERVES 8

Cut fettucine into 4-inch lengths. Cook and drain. Place in a large bowl, cover and chill.

Cut peppers into slices. Chop cauliflower into florets. Peel and slice carrots. Slice radishes into rounds. Cut mushrooms into quarters. Chop onion. Put vegetables into a pot of boiling water and blanch 5 to 6 minutes. Pour vegetables into colander and then plunge into ice water. When chilled, drain.

Mix remaining ingredients to make dressing. Toss fettucine with vegetables and dressing. Chill before serving.

Serving: 1/8 Recipe	Calories: 265	Protein: 8 gm
Calories from Fat: 77	Total Fat: 8.5 gm	Dietary Fiber: 3 gm
Saturated Fat: 1 gm	Carbs: 38 gm	Sodium: 43 mg
Component of Fat: 28%	Cholesterol: 37 mg	Calcium: 46 mg

Sweet & Sour Beets

3 cups fresh cooked or
   canned beets, peeled
   and sliced
$1/_2$ cup beet juice reserved
   from cooking or can
$1/_2$ cup herbed vinegar
3 tablespoons sugar
pinch of salt
1 small onion, peeled and
   stuck with 3 cloves
1 teaspoon white pepper
$1/_2$ bay leaf
$1/_2$ teaspoon prepared
   horseradish

SERVES 4

Place sliced beets in a 1-quart glass jar.

Boil beet juice with vinegar, then add remaining ingredients. Bring back to a boil, and simmer 10 minutes. Pour into beet jar. When cool, cover jar and refrigerate. Chill at least 12 hours before serving.

Serving: 1/4 Recipe
Calories from Fat: 4
Saturated Fat: 0 gm
Component of Fat: 3%

Calories: 107
Total Fat: .5 gm
Carbs: 26 gm
Cholesterol: 0 mg

Protein: 2 gm
Dietary Fiber: 3 gm
Sodium: 131 mg
Calcium: 29 mg

Hearts of Palm
with Romaine Lettuce

2 cans hearts of palm
1 head romaine lettuce
1 red pepper
4 teaspoons chopped
    parsley
4 pinches paprika

Serve with either:
Herbed Italian
    Vinaigrette, pg. 63
Parmesan Dressing, pg. 64

SERVES 4

Drain hearts of palm, and cut into lengthwise strips. Arrange romaine on 4 salad plates, and place hearts of palm over romaine.

Slice red pepper into strips, arrange on plates. Sprinkle 1 teaspoon parsley and a pinch of paprika on each salad.

Serve with your choice of dressing.

Serving: 1/4 Recipe
Calories from Fat: 4
Saturated Fat: 0 gm
Component of Fat: 2%

Calories: 167
Total Fat: .5 gm
Carbs: 42 gm
Cholesterol: 0 mg

Protein: 5 gm
Dietary Fiber: 3 gm
Sodium: 54 mg
Calcium: 41 mg

Hot Endive Salad

The tender white Belgian endives are grown without light. They can be home-grown in basements, or purchased fresh in the store year-round.

1 cup vegetable bouillon
  broth
8 Belgian endives

Serve with either:
Light Russian Dressing,
    page 64
Sweet Marjoram Italian
    Dressing, below

SERVES 4

Wash endives well, taking care to get out the grit between leaves. Briefly steam endives in broth until tender.

Cut off end of endives. Decoratively spread leaves of 2 endives on each salad plate. Serve while hot with dressing swirled over leaves.

Serving: 1/4 Recipe
Calories from Fat: 2
Saturated Fat: 0 gm
Component of Fat: 6%

Calories: 26
Total Fat: 0 gm
Carbs: 5 gm
Cholesterol: 0 mg

Protein: 1 gm
Dietary Fiber: 3 gm
Sodium: 43 mg
Calcium: 52 mg

Sweet Marjoram Dressing: This is an old-style herbal recipe with lots of flavor. Combine $1/4$ cup olive oil, $1/4$ cup white wine, $1/2$ cup cider vinegar, 2 teaspoons sweet marjoram, $1/2$ teaspoon garlic powder, 2 teaspoons Italian parsley, $1/2$ teaspoon paprika, salt and pepper to taste. Shake well. Refrigerate at least 3 hours. Makes 1 cup.

Arugula and Grapefruit Salad

Dressing:
$^1/_2$ cup unsweetened
    grapefruit juice
2 tablespoons Dijon
    mustard
2 tablespoons olive oil
1 teaspoon lemon juice
3 tablespoons honey
2 tablespoons poppy seeds
2 tablespoons finely
    grated onion
$^1/_2$ teaspoon black pepper
pinch of salt

4 packed cups torn
    arugula leaves
1 cup grapefruit sections

SERVES 4

In a small bowl, whisk together all dressing ingredients. Cover, and chill at least 2 hours to allow flavors to blend.

Just before serving, prepare and combine arugula leaves and grapefruit sections. Toss with desired amount of salad dressing.

Serving: 1/4 Recipe
Calories from Fat: 89
Saturated Fat: 1 gm
Component of Fat: 45%

Calories: 177
Total Fat: 9.5 gm
Carbs: 24 gm
Cholesterol: 0 mg

Protein: 2 gm
Dietary Fiber: 2 gm
Sodium: 79 mg
Calcium: 115 mg

Artichoke and Pimento Salad

This recipe is my mother's fabulous "might-as-well-make it-a-meal" salad. Everyone eats so much of it, there's no room left for anything else!

SERVES 8

2 cans artichoke hearts in
    water
½ cup thinly sliced
    pimento from canned
    whole pimentos
6 cups chopped leaf lettuce
½ cup grated Parmesan
    cheese
¼ cup olive oil
¼ cup red wine vinegar
2 cloves garlic, finely
    minced
2 tablespoons parsley
1 teaspoon sugar
salt and pepper to taste

Chill all ingredients. Drain and press liquid from artichokes, chop into bite-sized pieces. Combine in salad bowl with sliced pimento, lettuce and Parmesan cheese. Toss with remaining ingredients, adjust seasonings and vinegar to taste. Serve at once.

Serving: 1/8 Recipe	Calories: 97	Protein: 4 gm
Calories from Fat: 60	Total Fat: 6.5 gm	Dietary Fiber: 1 gm
Saturated Fat: 1.5 gm	Carbs: 5 gm	Sodium: 153 mg
Component of Fat: 62%	Cholesterol: 4 mg	Calcium: 103 mg

Nauset Light, Eastham, Massachusetts

Chilled Lobster Salad

2 cups cooked lobster
   meat, cut into bite-
   sized pieces
$^3/_2$ cup non-fat mayonnaise
1 tablespoon lemon juice
1 shallot, minced
2 tablespoons sweet relish
1 teaspoon chervil
1 teaspoon parsley
$^1/_4$ teaspoon white pepper
1 tablespoon capers

SERVES 4

Place lobster meat in refrigerator to chill.

Whisk together remaining ingredients. Pat lobster meat dry, then fold into sauce. Chill thoroughly before serving on a bed of lettuce or in a lobster roll.

Serving: 1/4 Recipe	Calories: 103	Protein: 15 gm
Calories from Fat: 4	Total Fat: .5 gm	Dietary Fiber: 0 gm
Saturated Fat: 0 gm	Carbs: 8 gm	Sodium: 547 mg
Component of Fat: 4%	Cholesterol: 52 mg	Calcium: 48 mg

Lobsters move about by darting backwards, using their abdomen and tail. Their shell is an external skeleton and is shed in the summer to grow a new one. Lobsters eat snails, clams, mussels, dead fish and even each other! Their large claw is used to crack shellfish, and the smaller claw for feeding. Deepwater lobsters can weigh up to 40 pounds.

Basil Tomato Aspic

SERVES 8

4 cups chopped canned
   tomatoes and juice
2 tablespoons lemon juice
1 teaspoon sugar
1 teaspoon paprika
1 tablespoon basil
1 bay leaf
2 tablespoons chopped
   onion
1/4 teaspoon celery salt
1/2 teaspoon white pepper
2 tablespoons gelatin
1/2 cup cold water

Garnish:
watercress

Simmer chopped tomatoes with their juice,
lemon juice, sugar, paprika, basil, bay leaf,
onion, celery salt and pepper for 30 minutes.

Soak gelatin in cold water. Stir into hot tomato
mixture until gelatin has dissolved. Allow to
thicken at room temperature.

Pour into wet mold. Chill until firm.

To unmold: Briefly set lower part of mold in
warm water. Turn onto platter lined with
watercress.

Serving: 1/8 Recipe	Calories: 37	Protein: 3 gm
Calories from Fat: 2	Total Fat: 0 gm	Dietary Fiber: 2 gm
Saturated Fat: 0 gm	Carbs: 7 gm	Sodium: 326 mg
Component of Fat: 4%	Cholesterol: 0 mg	Calcium: 49 mg

Billie's Congealed Salad

For a pot-luck bash of Blue Hill's Bagaduce Chorale, the consensus was to give Billie (a good-cookin' southern woman) some slack for this salad's name.

SERVES 8

1 pkg. lemon gelatin
1 pkg. lime gelatin
1 cup boiling water
1 can skimmed
    evaporated milk
1 cup non-fat mayonnaise
1 cup canned crushed
    pineapple, drained
1 cup non-fat cottage
    cheese

Optional:
$^1/_3$ cup chopped pecans
$^1/_3$ cup Maraschino
    cherries, drained

In a large bowl, pour boiling water over gelatins. Mix until dissolved. Add milk and mayonnaise and beat with whisk until smooth. Press moisture out of pineapple, then stir into gelatin with cottage cheese. If desired, add pecans and/or Maraschino cherries.

Pour gelatin into wet mold. Refrigerate until firm, preferably overnight. Unmold onto platter.

Serving: 1/8 Recipe   Calories: 77   Protein: 7 gm
Calories from Fat: 1   Total Fat: 0 gm   Dietary Fiber: 0 gm
Saturated Fat: 0 gm   Carbs: 11 gm   Sodium: 341 mg
Component of Fat: 2%   Cholesterol: 1 mg   Calcium: 109 mg

Herbed Italian Vinaigrette

$^1/_2$ cup white wine vinegar
3 cloves garlic, sliced
1 teaspoon oregano
1 teaspoon basil
1 teaspoon dill
$^1/_2$ cup vegetable broth
$^1/_4$ cup olive oil
1 tablespoon lemon juice
1 tablespoon grated
    Parmesan cheese
$^1/_2$ teaspoon pepper

MAKES 1$^1/_4$ CUPS

Simmer vinegar in uncovered stainless-steel pot with garlic, oregano, basil, dill and broth for 15 minutes. Transfer into blender and add olive oil, lemon juice, Parmesan and pepper. Process about 1 minute. Chill well.

Serving: 2 Tablespoons	Calories: 54	Protein: 0 gm
Calories from Fat: 50	Total Fat: 5.5 gm	Dietary Fiber: 0 gm
Saturated Fat: 1 gm	Carbs: 1 gm	Sodium: 14 mg
Component of Fat: 89%	Cholesterol: 0 mg	Calcium: 15 mg

Curried Dijon Salad Sauce

2 teaspoons gelatin
2 tablespoons cold water
1 cup vegetable broth
1 teaspoon sugar
1 tablespoon lemon juice
1 tablespoon curry powder
$^1/_4$ cup Dijon mustard

MAKES 1$^1/_4$ CUPS

Soak gelatin in cold water. Boil vegetable broth and add to gelatin mixture. Stir in remaining ingredients. Chill. Before serving dressing, beat with a wire whisk.

Serving: 2 Tablespoons	Calories: 16	Protein: 1 gm
Calories from Fat: 5	Total Fat: .5 gm	Dietary Fiber: 0 gm
Saturated Fat: 0 gm	Carbs: 2 gm	Sodium: 43 mg
Component of Fat: 28%	Cholesterol: 0 mg	Calcium: 11 mg

Parmesan Dressing

1/2 cup low-fat buttermilk
1/2 cup non-fat sour cream
2 tablespoons white wine
    vinegar
1/3 cup grated Parmesan
    cheese
1 teaspoon garlic, minced
1/2 teaspoon white pepper

MAKES 1 CUP

Whisk all ingredients together until well blended. Chill before serving.

Serving: 2 Tablespoons	Calories: 40	Protein: 9 gm
Calories from Fat: 16	Total Fat: 2 gm	Dietary Fiber: 0 gm
Saturated Fat: 1.5 gm	Carbs: 4 gm	Sodium: 168 mg
Component of Fat: 24%	Cholesterol: 3 mg	Calcium: 85 mg

Thousand Island Dressing

1/2 cup non-fat plain yogurt
1/2 cup non-fat mayonnaise
1/2 cup non-fat cottage
    cheese
1 clove garlic, minced
1 teaspoon pepper
1/3 cup chili sauce
1/4 cup lemon juice
1/4 cup pickle relish

MAKES 2 1/4 CUPS

Combine yogurt, mayonnaise, cottage cheese, garlic and pepper in blender. Process until smooth. Transfer into bowl and whisk in remaining ingredients. Chill.

Serving: 2 Tablespoons	Calories: 24	Protein: 1 gm
Calories from Fat: 0	Total Fat: 0 gm	Dietary Fiber: 0 gm
Saturated Fat: 0 gm	Carbs: 5 gm	Sodium: 184 mg
Component of Fat: 2%	Cholesterol: 0 mg	Calcium: 16 mg

Soups,
Stews
and
Chowders

CONTENTS

COASTAL NEW ENGLAND   WINTERFARE COOKING

Freeport Shrimp Étouffé

SERVES 6

1 tablespoon safflower oil
1 cup chopped yellow
    onion
1 cup chopped green
    pepper
2 cloves garlic, minced
1 cup vegetable bouillon
    broth
1$\frac{1}{2}$ cups chopped stewed
    tomatoes and their juice
1 teaspoon thyme
1 teaspoon saffron
1 bay leaf
$\frac{1}{2}$ teaspoon Tabasco sauce
1$\frac{1}{2}$ lbs. shrimp, cooked,
    peeled and deveined
3 tablespoons chopped
    parsley
$\frac{1}{4}$ cup skim milk
6 cups boiled rice

In a large skillet, heat oil, sauté onion, pepper and garlic. Add bouillon broth, tomatoes and their juice, thyme, saffron, bay leaf and Tabasco sauce. Cover, simmer 10 minutes.

Squeeze shrimp dry in a cloth towel, chop into small pieces, and stir in. Simmer 25 minutes. Remove from heat, add parsley and milk. Let set 5 minutes, then stir. Serve over boiled rice.

Serving: 1/6 Recipe	Calories: 385	Protein: 30 gm
Calories from Fat: 39	Total Fat: 4.5 gm	Dietary Fiber: 2 gm
Saturated Fat: .5 gm	Carbs: 54 gm	Sodium: 435 mg
Component of Fat: 10%	Cholesterol: 222 mg	Calcium: 125 mg

Curried Butternut Soup

1 tablespoon sweet butter
2 tablespoons sherry or
    vermouth
2 cups chopped yellow
    onions
2 large butternut squash
1 tablespoon curry
1 teaspoon nutmeg
$2^{1}/_{4}$ cups vegetable bouillon
    broth
1 cup apple juice
2 McIntosh apples,
    peeled and grated
$^{1}/_{4}$ teaspoon pepper

Serve with:
non-fat sour cream

SERVES 6

In a large pot, melt butter with sherry or vermouth over low heat. Add chopped onions, cover and cook until clear, about 20 minutes.

Peel squash, remove seeds and cut into 1-inch cubes. Add squash and remaining ingredients to pot. Simmer 30 minutes.

Strain soup. Put solids into blender with 2 cups strained liquid. Process until smooth. Return to pot and mix in remaining strained liquid until soup is of desired consistency. Heat 10 minutes. Serve with sour cream.

Serving: 1/6 Recipe
Calories from Fat: 28
Saturated Fat: 1.5 gm
Component of Fat: 16%

Calories: 154
Total Fat: 3 gm
Carbs: 32 gm
Cholesterol: 5 mg

Protein: 3 gm
Dietary Fiber: 7 gm
Sodium: 433 mg
Calcium: 78 mg

COASTAL NEW ENGLAND   WINTERFARE COOKING

Clear Mushroom Soup

4 cups vegetable bouillon broth
1 lb. mushrooms
1/4 cup sherry
2 tablespoons chopped parsley

SERVES 4

Bring bouillon broth to a boil. Wash and slice mushrooms to show their shape. Add mushrooms and sherry to bouillon and simmer 15 minutes. Clear Mushroom Soup may be served hot or cold. Garnish with parsley.

Serving: 1/4 Recipe
Calories from Fat: 4
Saturated Fat: 0 gm
Component of Fat: 5%

Calories: 77
Total Fat: .5 gm
Carbs: 13 gm
Cholesterol: 0 mg

Protein: 3 gm
Dietary Fiber: 1 gm
Sodium: 173 mg
Calcium: 9 mg

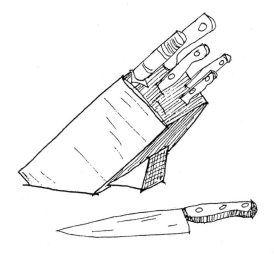

Creamy Corn Clam Chowder

12 large quahog clams or
   36 littlenecks
2 cups boiling water
1 medium-sized onion,
   chopped fine
1 teaspoon butter
2 cups peeled and diced
   potatoes
$1/_4$ teaspoon salt
1 teaspoon black pepper
3 cups skim milk blended
   with 1 cup non-fat
   powdered milk
1 tablespoon flour
1 cup pre-cooked corn
   kernels

SERVES 4

Scrub clams discarding any that do not close. Steam 20 minutes in boiling water. Strain clam juice through very fine sieve and reserve.

Sauté onion in butter. Add potatoes, spices, milk and 1 cup reserved clam juice. Cover and simmer on medium heat until potatoes are soft. Transfer cooked mixture to blender. With blender running, add flour and process until smooth. Pour back into pot, cook 5 minutes.

Shuck clams and coarsely chop meat. Add clams and corn to chowder, cook 3 minutes.

Serving: 1/4 Recipe	Calories: 455	Protein: 45 gm
Calories from Fat: 37	Total Fat: 4 gm	Dietary Fiber: 4 gm
Saturated Fat: 1 gm	Carbs: 59 gm	Sodium: 483 mg
Component of Fat: 8%	Cholesterol: 85 mg	Calcium: 564 mg

Soft-shell clams are mostly found north of Cape Cod, and are commonly called steamers. Hard-shell clams include the quahogs and littleneck clams, which are the most popular clams in New England. Wash clams several times to rinse out all the sand. Whether in the shell or shucked, clams should be plump and fresh-smelling.

Lazyman's Lobster Stew

Cooked meat of 2 lobsters
    cut into bite-sized
    pieces, about 2 cups
2 teaspoons butter
$\frac{1}{2}$ cup vermouth
$3\frac{1}{2}$ cups skim milk
    blended with $1\frac{1}{2}$ cups
    non-fat powdered milk
$\frac{1}{2}$ teaspoon pepper

SERVES 4

Sauté lobster meat in butter. Add vermouth and simmer 5 minutes. Stir in remaining ingredients and heat, but do not boil.

Serving: 1/4 Recipe	Calories: 271	Protein: 30 gm
Calories from Fat: 27	Total Fat: 3 gm	Dietary Fiber: 0 gm
Saturated Fat: 1.5 gm	Carbs: 23 gm	Sodium: 524 mg
Component of Fat: 10%	Cholesterol: 65 mg	Calcium: 575 mg

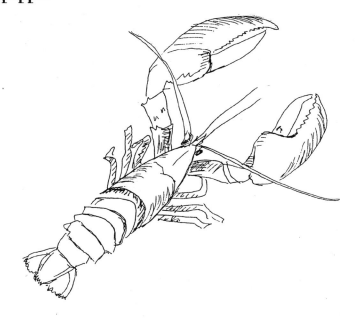

COASTAL NEW ENGLAND   WINTERFARE COOKING

Nantucket Seafood Chowder

*A medley of favorite seafood, Nantucket Seafood Chowder
makes a warming meal on a wintery day.*

2 teaspoons butter
2 cloves garlic, minced
1 cup chopped onion
1³/₄ cups clam juice
2 cups potatoes,
     peeled and diced
1 cup sea scallops
1 lb. flounder fillets
1 cup lobster meat
3 cups skim milk
¹/₂ cup skimmed
     evaporated milk
1 tablespoon parsley
pinch of nutmeg
salt and pepper to taste

SERVES 6

In a large pot sauté garlic with onion in butter until clear. Add clam juice and potatoes. Cover and simmer until potatoes are tender.

Cut sea scallops and flounder into bite-sized pieces. Add scallops, flounder and lobster meat to pot. Simmer 10 minutes.

Reduce heat and add remaining ingredients. Heat well, but do not boil.

Serving: 1/6 Recipe   Calories: 281   Protein: 35 gm
Calories from Fat: 29   Total Fat: 3 gm   Dietary Fiber: 2 gm
Saturated Fat: 1.5 gm   Carbs: 27 gm   Sodium: 496 mg
Component of Fat: 11%   Cholesterol: 83 mg   Calcium: 259 mg

Cheddar Chowder

SERVES 4

$^1/_2$ cup chopped onion
$^1/_2$ cup chopped celery
$^1/_2$ cup chopped carrots
1 tablespoon safflower oil
1 tablespoon sherry
$^1/_4$ cup flour
1 teaspoon paprika
1 teaspoon white pepper
2 cups vegetable bouillon
   broth
2 cups skim milk blended
   with 1 cup non-fat
   powdered milk
$^3/_4$ cup grated low-fat
   Cheddar cheese
1 tablespoon parsley

Cook onion, celery and carrots in oil until tender, but not brown. Blend in sherry, flour, paprika and pepper. Whisk in bouillon broth and milk.

Stirring constantly, cook over medium heat until thick and bubbly. Slowly stir in grated cheese and parsley.

Serving: 1/4 Recipe	Calories: 304	Protein: 27 gm
Calories from Fat: 76	Total Fat: 8.5 gm	Dietary Fiber: 2 gm
Saturated Fat: 2.5 gm	Carbs: 30 gm	Sodium: 358 mg
Component of Fat: 25%	Cholesterol: 20 mg	Calcium: 830 mg

Stamford Crab Bisque

1 lb. cooked crab meat
3 tablespoons grated
    onion
1 clove garlic, halved
$\frac{1}{2}$ cup sliced mushrooms
3 cups skim milk
1 cup clam juice
1 tablespoon butter
3 tablespoons flour
$\frac{1}{2}$ teaspoon white pepper
pinch of mace
pinch of salt

SERVES 4

Pick through crab meat to be sure all shell pieces have been removed.

On medium heat, simmer onion, garlic and mushrooms in milk and clam juice for 25 minutes, stirring frequently.

Heat butter in a saucepan, remove from heat and blend in flour to make a roux. Strain milk into roux, discarding vegetables. Return to heat and whisk bisque until thick and smooth. Stir in white pepper, mace and salt. Gently fold crab into bisque. Heat, but do not boil.

Serving: 1/4 Recipe	Calories: 234	Protein: 30 gm
Calories from Fat: 49	Total Fat: 5.5 gm	Dietary Fiber: 0 gm
Saturated Fat: 2.5 gm	Carbs: 15 gm	Sodium: 611 mg
Component of Fat: 21%	Cholesterol: 125 mg	Calcium: 350 mg

In 1640, the Siwanoys Indians sold the land, now called Stamford, to the New Haven Colony. A settlement was begun there the following year. Located on a wide bay crossed by two tidal inlets, Stamford is home to the Bartlett Arboretum, a branch of the Whitney Museum of Art, and a 30,000 square-foot store of New England antiques.

Creamy Potato Leek Soup

SERVES 4

8 medium-sized potatoes
3 leeks, white stalks only
5 cups water
$\frac{1}{2}$ teaspoon salt
$\frac{1}{2}$ teaspoon pepper
skim milk, optional

Peel and quarter potatoes. Wash leeks thoroughly and cut stalks into 1-inch rounds. Place potatoes, leeks and water in covered pot. Simmer until vegetables are very tender, at least 2 hours. Process potatoes, leeks and their water through food mill (or food processor, but texture will be bland). Stir in salt and pepper. If desired, thin with a little milk. Warm over low heat before serving.

Serving: 1/4 Recipe	Calories: 289	Protein: 6 gm
Calories from Fat: 5	Total Fat: .5 gm	Dietary Fiber: 7 gm
Saturated Fat: 0 gm	Carbs: 67 gm	Sodium: 332 mg
Component of Fat: 2%	Cholesterol: 0 mg	Calcium: 84 mg

Squash & Lentil Soup

2 cups red lentils
6 cups vegetable bouillon
    broth
1 cup white wine
1 cup chopped onion
1 cup peeled and diced
    carrots
1 cup diced celery
1 teaspoon thyme
2 teaspoons lemon juice
1 bay leaf
2 cups peeled acorn
    squash, diced into
    1-inch cubes
salt and pepper to taste

SERVES 6

Rinse lentils in cold water. Combine all ingredients, except squash, in a large covered pot. Stirring occasionally, simmer 1 hour, adding water if needed. Add squash and simmer another hour. Discard bay leaf. Adjust seasonings to taste.

Serving: 1/6 Recipe   Calories: 338   Protein: 20 gm
Calories from Fat: 7   Total Fat: 1 gm   Dietary Fiber: 24 gm
Saturated Fat: 0 gm   Carbs: 60 gm   Sodium: 137 mg
Component of Fat: 2%   Cholesterol: 0 mg   Calcium: 89 mg

Rosemary Minestrone

Rosemary Minestrone is outstanding served with Parmesan or pesto.

1 cup small white beans
2 tablespoons olive oil
1 cup thin onion slivers
2 cloves garlic, minced
2 cups vegetable broth
6 cups water
2 cups grated cabbage
2 cups diced potatoes
1 cup chopped celery
2 cups diced zucchini
1 cup cut frozen green
   beans
2 cups chopped peeled
   plum tomatoes
2 tablespoons grated
   lemon rind
1 cup dry spaghetti,
   broken into pieces
1 teaspoon salt
1 teaspoon pepper
2 tablespoons rosemary
$\frac{1}{4}$ cup chopped parsley

SERVES 8

Wash and soak beans overnight in cold water. In the morning, rinse, and drain.

In a large pot, sauté onion and garlic in olive oil until soft, but not brown. Add beans, broth, water, cabbage, potatoes and celery. Bring to a boil, reduce heat and cover pot. Simmer 2 hours. Add remaining ingredients and cook another 30 minutes.

Serving: 1/8 Recipe
Calories from Fat: 40
Saturated Fat: .5 gm
Component of Fat: 15%

Calories: 253
Total Fat: 4.5 gm
Carbs: 45 gm
Cholesterol: 0 mg

Protein: 11 gm
Dietary Fiber: 8 gm
Sodium: 353 mg
Calcium: 123 mg

Cream of Cauliflower

5 medium-sized potatoes
1 medium-sized head of
   cauliflower
2 cups chopped yellow
   onions
4 cups water
$^1/_2$ teaspoon salt
$^1/_2$ teaspoon pepper
skim milk, optional

SERVES 4

Peel and quarter potatoes. Cut cauliflower and stalks. Place potatoes, cauliflower, onion and water in covered pot. Simmer until very soft. Process vegetables and cooking water through food mill (or food processor, but texture will be bland). Stir in salt and pepper. If desired, thin with a little milk.

Serving: 1/4 Recipe	Calories: 205	Protein: 6 gm
Calories from Fat: 8	Total Fat: 1 gm	Dietary Fiber: 8 gm
Saturated Fat: 0 gm	Carbs: 46 gm	Sodium: 327 mg
Component of Fat: 4%	Cholesterol: 0 mg	Calcium: 55 mg

New Englanders get through winter "cabin-fever" by creating special events and attractions. The Mystic Valley Railway offers a Snowflake Special from Boston to the Berkshires, Boston also hosts the Sleigh Bell Parade and Reenactment of the Boston Tea Party. Mystic Seaport decorates in scenes of Christmases past.

Ratatouille Stew

2 cups peeled and diced
    eggplant
$1/_2$ teaspoon salt
1 tablespoon olive oil
2 cloves garlic, minced
1 cup thinly sliced onion
$1/_2$ cup thinly sliced red or
    green pepper
2 cups peeled and chopped
    plum tomatoes and
    their juice
2 teaspoons brown sugar
1 cup vegetable broth
2 cups chopped zucchini
2 teaspoons oregano
1 tablespoon lemon juice
2 tablespoons basil
3 tablespoons parsley
2 teaspoons pepper

Optional:
non-fat sour-cream

SERVES 6

Toss eggplant with salt to remove excess moisture. Put in collander to drain over bowl.

Heat olive oil. Sauté eggplant with garlic, onion and peppers. Stir in tomatoes and juice, brown sugar, vegetable broth, zucchini, oregano, lemon juice, basil, parsley and pepper. Simmer 10 minutes.

Add drained liquid from eggplant to stew. Cover pot, simmer over medium heat 30 minutes. Uncover pot and simmer 30 minutes more. Adjust seasonings to taste. If desired, serve with sour cream.

Serving: 1/6 Recipe	Calories: 97	Protein: 3 gm
Calories from Fat: 26	Total Fat: 3 gm	Dietary Fiber: 4 gm
Saturated Fat: .5 gm	Carbs: 17 gm	Sodium: 236 mg
Component of Fat: 24%	Cholesterol: 0 mg	Calcium: 67 mg

Matelote Stew

This celebration of freshwater fish originated in the Mediterranean region, and was adapted to suit the freshwater fish of New England.

12 small pearl onions
$^1/_2$ lb. mushrooms
$^1/_2$ lb. small salad shrimp,
    peeled
1 tablespoon olive oil
2 lbs. freshwater fish, such
    as perch, trout, carp
3 cups dry red wine
$1^1/_2$ cups fish stock or broth
$1^1/_2$ cups water
1 tablespoon parsley
$^1/_2$ cup chopped celery
1 bay leaf
2 cloves garlic
1 teaspoon thyme
1 teaspoon salt
1 teaspoon pepper
2 tablespoons warm
    brandy
$1^1/_2$ tablespoons butter
3 tablespoons flour

SERVES 6

Peel and cut pearl onions in half. Slice mushrooms. Wash shrimp. Sauté onions, mushrooms and shrimp in oil over low heat. Prepare the soup while this garnish cooks.

Clean and cut freshwater fish into bite-sized pieces. Place in pot with red wine, stock or broth, and water. Add parsley, celery, bay leaf, garlic, thyme, salt and pepper. Bring to a boil, then reduce heat and simmer 5 minutes.

Remove pot from heat. Float warm brandy on top, and ignite. When flame burns out, return to stove, simmer 15 minutes. With a slotted spoon, transfer fish to oven dish, cover and keep warm. Make a roux of butter, flour and $^1/_4$ cup of the prepared broth. Whisk into broth, heat to thicken, but do not boil. Put fish into soup bowls, cover with shrimp garnish and ladle stewed sauce on top.

Serving: 1/4 Recipe	Calories: 103	Protein: 15 gm
Calories from Fat: 4	Total Fat: .5 gm	Dietary Fiber: 0 gm
Saturated Fat: 0 gm	Carbs: 8 gm	Sodium: 547 mg
Component of Fat: 4%	Cholesterol: 52 mg	Calcium: 48 mg

Main Meal Dishes

CONTENTS

Any fish, cooked by any means, generally requires only 10 minutes of cooking time for each inch of thickness, measured at its thickest part.

COASTAL NEW ENGLAND   WINTERFARE COOKING

Oven-Fried Ipswich Clams

Ispwich clams come out of the Essex River in Massachusetts. If possible, use real Ipswich clams, famous for their lucious flavor and tenderness.

3 cups raw shucked clams,
    Ipswich or littleneck
1 tablespoon canola oil
2 egg whites
1 cup flour
1 teaspoon salt
1 teaspoon pepper
1 teaspoon paprika
1 teaspoon dried parsley

SERVES 4

Preheat oven to 400°. Spray a baking pan with 3 coats of non-stick oil. Pat dry the shucked clams in a towel.

In a small bowl, combine oil and egg whites together with about 15 strokes. In a separate bowl, mix flour and spices.

Dip clams in liquid mixture, then coat in herbed flour. Shake off extra flour in sieve, then place on wax paper until flour is absorbed by moisture.

Place clams in a single layer on prepared baking pan, set on lowest rack of oven. After 5 minutes, flip clams to brown on other side. Bake until browned and crispy. Serve hot.

Serving: 1/4 Recipe	Calories: 230	Protein: 19 gm
Calories from Fat: 44	Total Fat: 5 gm	Dietary Fiber: 1 gm
Saturated Fat: .5 gm	Carbs: 26 gm	Sodium: 383 mg
Component of Fat: 19%	Cholesterol: 39 mg	Calcium: 65 mg

COASTAL NEW ENGLAND   WINTERFARE COOKING

Wicked Good Lobster Feast

2 cups white wine
6 dozen steamer clams
12 small red potatoes
6 lobsters, 1-1$\frac{1}{2}$ lbs. each
6 ears of corn, husked

Butter-Wine Sauce:
3 tablespoons hot melted
    butter
1$\frac{1}{2}$ cup strained poaching
    wine from steamed
    lobster/clams
2 tablespoons lemon juice

SERVES 6

Pour wine into 24-quart steamer pot. Cover and heat until it steams.

Scrub clams, discarding any with broken shells or that do not close tightly when handled. Tie clams by the dozen, in squares of cheesecloth tied with string. Allow room in bags for clams to open.

Place potatoes in covered pot. 10 minutes later, add lobsters and corn. After 15 minutes, add steamer bags. Steam clams until they open, about 12 minutes. In a saucepan, combine ingredients for Butter-Wine Sauce, simmer 10 minutes. Serve in dipping bowls.

Serving: 1/6 Recipe	Calories: 448	Protein: 44 gm
Calories from Fat: 47	Total Fat: 5 gm	Dietary Fiber: 4 gm
Saturated Fat: 2 gm	Carbs: 44 gm	Sodium: 639 mg
Component of Fat: 10%	Cholesterol: 138 mg	Calcium: 143 mg

COASTAL NEW ENGLAND   WINTERFARE COOKING

How to Eat
Lobster and Clams

Lobster: Bend back claws and flippers, break off where attached to body. Use cracker and pick to remove meat in claws and knuckles. Suck meat from flippers.

Bend back tail and break off from body. Tail flippers can also be broken back and the meat pushed out, or you can cut the membrane. In the body is the green tomalley (liver) and the red coral of the females (roe).

Clams: Wedge open shells and loosen meat. Dip in broth to rinse off sand.

COASTAL NEW ENGLAND   WINTERFARE COOKING

Pan-Fried Tuna Steaks

4 tuna steaks, sized to
    suit appetites
1 cup flour
2 teaspoons paprika
2 teaspoons tarragon
2 teaspoons pepper
$1/2$ teaspoon salt
1 teaspoon garlic powder
2 egg whites
2 tablespoons olive oil

SERVES 4

Preheat frying pan on medium-high heat.

Combine flour and spices in a mixing bowl. In a separate bowl, whisk egg whites until frothy. Dip tuna steaks in egg whites, then in spiced flour. Shake off excess flour and place on wax paper.

Spray hot frying pan with non-stick oil and coat pan with olive oil. When oil is hot, fry tuna steaks, nicely browning on each side. Check to see that inside of steaks are cooked, they should be opaque, not translucent.

Serving: 1 Steak	Calories: 320	Protein: 30 gm
Calories from Fat: 96	Total Fat: 10.5 gm	Dietary Fiber: 1 gm
Saturated Fat: 2 gm	Carbs: 24 gm	Sodium: 361 mg
Component of Fat: 31%	Cholesterol: 40 mg	Calcium: 24 mg

COASTAL NEW ENGLAND   WINTERFARE COOKING

Shrimp Kebabs in Beer Marinade

1 1/2 lbs. medium-sized
   raw shrimp (41-50
   count) peeled and
   deveined
1/2 cup pre-cooked,
   canned pearl onions
12 cherry tomatoes
1 can light beer
1 tablespoon parsley
1 tablespoon basil
1 teaspoon minced garlic
2 teaspoons dry mustard
1 tablespoon lemon juice
1 teaspoon pepper
1/2 teaspoon ground celery
   seeds

Serve with:
3 cups cooked rice

SERVES 4

Clean, rinse and dry shrimp. Place shrimp, pearl onions and tomatoes in mixing bowl.

In a separate bowl, mix together remaining ingredients. Pour over shrimp and vegetables. Cover and chill until ready to broil.

Preheat broiler. Arrange shrimp, pearl onions and tomatoes on flat, double edged skewers. Rest ends of skewers on lips of baking pan, to catch the drippings. Place on rack nearest broiler, turn skewers and baste after 4 minutes. Broil 3-4 minutes on second side and baste again. Serve on bed of rice.

Serving: 1/4 Recipe	Calories: 383	Protein: 41 gm
Calories from Fat: 26	Total Fat: 3 gm	Dietary Fiber: 2 gm
Saturated Fat: .5 gm	Carbs: 41 gm	Sodium: 392 mg
Component of Fat: 7%	Cholesterol: 332 mg	Calcium: 130 mg

Coquilles St. Jacques

SERVES 4

1¹/₂ lbs. scallops, whole if small, quartered or halved if large
1 cup dry vermouth
1 bay leaf
1 teaspoon butter
2 tablespoons white wine
3 tablespoons flour
³/₄ cup skim milk blended with ¹/₄ cup non-fat powdered milk
pinch of salt
¹/₂ teaspoon white pepper
¹/₂ teaspoon freshly squeezed lemon juice
¹/₂ cup grated low-fat Swiss Lorraine cheese

Prepare scallops: Boil vermouth with bay leaf. Poach the scallops in the boiling liquid for 2 minutes, remove pot from heat but leave in hot liquid 10 minutes more. With a slotted spoon, transfer scallops to a bowl. Remove bay leaf, boil down poaching liquid to 1 cup.

In a saucepan, heat butter and white wine. Blend in flour, cook 1 minute. Remove from heat and whisk in milk, poaching liquid, salt and pepper. Simmer and stir over medium heat. If too thick, add a little milk.

Remove sauce from heat, stir in lemon juice. Fold into scallops and transfer to baking dish. Sprinkle with grated cheese. Just before serving, place 5 inches under broiler until bubbly and light brown.

Serving: 1/4 Recipe	Calories: 365	Protein: 40 gm
Calories from Fat: 76	Total Fat: 8.5 gm	Dietary Fiber: 0 gm
Saturated Fat: 5 gm	Carbs: 14 gm ·	Sodium: 503 mg
Component of Fat: 21%	Cholesterol: 80 mg	Calcium: 357 mg

Smoked Trout Mousse

This mousse makes a cool showing at a holiday buffet or potluck.

2 cups part-skim Ricotta
   cheese
3 tablespoons prepared
   horseradish
1 tablespoon finely
   chopped green onion
2 tablespoons prepared
   sweet mustard
$^1/_4$ teaspoon salt
$^1/_2$ teaspoon pepper
$^1/_2$ lb. flaked smoked trout

Serve on:
salad greens with lemon

SERVES 6

In a food processor or blender, purée Ricotta until completely smooth. Transfer to mixing bowl and blend in horseradish, chopped green onion, mustard, salt and pepper. Fold in flaked trout and gently mix well.

Place mixture into wet 1-quart fish (or other-shaped) mold. Chill at least 6 hours before serving. Unmold trout mousse on a bed of greens decorated with lemon slices.

Serving: 1/6 Recipe	Calories: 179	Protein: 19 gm
Calories from Fat: 77	Total Fat: 8.5 gm	Dietary Fiber: 0 gm
Saturated Fat: 5 gm	Carbs: 6 gm	Sodium: 533 mg
Component of Fat: 44%	Cholesterol: 41 mg	Calcium: 240 mg

The potluck was born of necessity. Barn-raisings and other events requiring a community spirit always went best with food. Potlucks today are also an easy way to gather friends and family for a meal, a holiday, or special celebration, and to share the offering of food. The only potluck rule is to bring plenty, especially if your cooking is good!

COASTAL NEW ENGLAND   WINTERFARE COOKING

Frenchman's Bay
Baked Stuffed Lobster

5 live lobsters, 1-1½ lbs.
1 teaspoon butter
3 tablespoons chopped
    shallots
2 cloves garlic, minced
½ cup sherry
2 tablespoons balsamic
    vinegar
1 tablespoon lemon juice
3 tablespoons parsley
1 teaspoon pepper
1½ cups bread crumbs
2 tablespoons canola oil

SERVES 4

Steam lobsters in a large covered pot in 2 inches boiling water. Lobsters will be cooked in 20-25 minutes, depending on their size. Remove lobsters and reserve a cup of the liquid. Remove the tail and claw meat from the smallest lobster and chop it into small pieces.

Heat butter in saucepan. Sauté shallots and garlic. Add sherry, vinegar, lemon juice, the cup of reserved liquid, parsley and pepper. Stir in bread crumbs, then chopped lobster meat.

Split the other 4 lobsters down the underside of the body. Clean out the bodies, adding the green tomalley and red coral to the bread crumb mixture, if desired. Fill the lobster bodies with the stuffing. Brush shells with canola oil and place on baking sheet. Bake in preheated 400° oven 20 minutes.

Serving: 1 Lobster	Calories: 258	Protein: 31 gm
Calories from Fat: 24	Total Fat: 2.5 gm	Dietary Fiber: 1 gm
Saturated Fat: 1 gm	Carbs: 18 gm	Sodium: 642 mg
Component of Fat: 10%	Cholesterol: 105 mg	Calcium: 122 mg

COASTAL NEW ENGLAND   WINTERFARE COOKING

Simple Fillet of Sole Bon Femme

8 equal-sized fillets of sole
2 cups sliced mushrooms
1 cup white wine
2 teaspoons butter
$^3/_4$ cup skim milk blended
    with $^1/_4$ cup non-fat
    powdered milk
1 tablespoon flour
2 teaspoons tarragon
salt and pepper to taste
1 teaspoon lemon juice

SERVES 4

Preheat oven to 400°. Spray baking pan with non-stick oil.

Place 4 fillets in pan, cover with mushrooms, then place second fillet over mushrooms. Pour wine in pan.   Poach in oven 20 minutes. Remove pan and drain juices into saucepan.

To cooking juice in saucepan, whisk in butter, milk, flour, tarragon, salt and pepper. Rapidly boil down until consistency of heavy cream. Remove from heat and stir in lemon juice. Spread sauce over fillets. Return to oven 6-7 minutes, to heat through.

Serving: 1/4 Recipe
Calories from Fat: 45
Saturated Fat: 2 gm
Component of Fat: 15%

Calories: 307
Total Fat: 5 gm
Carbs: 8 gm
Cholesterol: 123 mg

Protein: 45 gm
Dietary Fiber: 1 gm
Sodium: 280 mg
Calcium: 157 mg

COASTAL NEW ENGLAND   WINTERFARE COOKING

Fancy Flounder
with Piquant Tomato Sauce

2$\frac{1}{2}$ lbs. flounder fillets
1$\frac{1}{2}$ cups white wine
1 cup chopped yellow
   onion
1 tablespoon olive oil
1 tablespoon lemon juice
1 teaspoon oregano
2 tablespoons tiny capers
3 cups peeled tomatoes,
   finely chopped,
   with their juices
1 tablespoon butter

SERVES 6

Preheat oven to 350°. Place flounder in an oven dish and pour wine over fish. Poach in oven just until cooked through. Drain liquid and set aside. Cover fish to keep warm.

In a saucepan, sauté onion in olive oil. When onion is clear, add lemon juice, oregano, capers, and tomatoes with juice. Rapidly boil down until sauce is very thick. Reduce heat.

Add poaching liquid to tomato sauce. Rapidly boil down until about 3 cups remain. Stir in butter. Serve immediately with Piquant Tomato Sauce spooned over flounder.

Serving: 1/6 Recipe	Calories: 343	Protein: 47 gm
Calories from Fat: 70	Total Fat: 7.5 gm	Dietary Fiber: 2 gm
Saturated Fat: 2.5 gm	Carbs: 10 gm	Sodium: 341 mg
Component of Fat: 21%	Cholesterol: 134 mg	Calcium: 57 mg

To trim your Christmas tree New England style, string popcorn and cranberries into ropes. Tree trimmings might include a small bird's nest, toy sail boats, miniature lobster pots and buoys. An old quilt makes a lovely tree skirt. For an old-fashioned Christmas Eve, plan a lights-out party, with only candlelight and the lights of the tree shining.

Cranberry Stuffed Rockport Haddock

2¹/₂ lbs. haddock fillets
1 tablespoon canola oil
¹/₂ cup chopped onion
1 tablespoon lemon juice
1 cup cleaned cranberries,
    fresh or frozen
¹/₂ cup brown sugar
¹/₂ cup orange juice
2 tablespoons parsley
2 cups cooked white or
    brown rice
1 egg, beaten
1 teaspoon canola oil
1 teaspoon paprika

SERVES 6

Spray a large casserole with non-stick oil. Place half the fillets on bottom of casserole.

Sauté onion in a tablespoon of oil. Add lemon juice, cranberries, brown sugar and orange juice. Simmer 25 minutes.

In a mixing bowl, combine cranberry sauce with parsley, cooked rice and beaten egg. Spread mixture over haddock fillets. Place remaining fillets over cranberry mixture. Brush fillets with oil, sprinkle with paprika.

Bake 35 minutes in preheated 350° oven.

Serving: 1/6 Recipe	Calories: 365	Protein: 39 gm
Calories from Fat: 51	Total Fat: 5.5 gm	Dietary Fiber: 1 gm
Saturated Fat: 1 gm	Carbs: 38 gm	Sodium: 150 mg
Component of Fat: 14%	Cholesterol: 143 mg	Calcium: 104 mg

Codfish Balls

1 lb. salt codfish
3 cups fish bouillon broth
3 medium-sized potatoes,
    cut into quarters
2 teaspoons grated lemon
    rind
$1/4$ cup grated onion
$1/2$ cup pre-cooked corn
    kernels
pinch of cayenne
1 teaspoon pepper
2 eggs
1 tablespoon skim milk
3 tablespoons flour
4 tablespoons safflower oil
prepared tartare or
    seafood sauce

SERVES 4

Soak salted codfish in cold water for 6 hours, rinsing and changing the water every hour.

Bring bouillon broth and potatoes to a boil. Simmer until potatoes are tender. Wrap desalted codfish in a cheesecloth and place in broth. Simmer 5 minutes, then remove pot from heat. Leave fish in hot broth another 5-10 minutes depending on thickness of fish. Remove codfish from cheesecloth and pat dry. Put codfish in bowl and use two forks to flake into shreds. In a separate bowl, mash potatoes. Stir potatoes, lemon rind, onion, corn, cayenne, pepper, eggs, milk and flour into codfish. Form into 1-inch balls.

Preheat and spray a frying pan with non-stick oil. Coat pan with safflower oil, and fry codfish balls until browned. Serve with tartare or seafood sauce.

Serving: 1/4 Recipe	Calories: 569	Protein: 80 gm
Calories from Fat: 110	Total Fat: 12 gm	Dietary Fiber: 3 gm
Saturated Fat: 1.5 gm	Carbs: 30 gm	Sodium: 234 mg
Component of Fat: 20%	Cholesterol: 106 mg	Calcium: 49 mg

COASTAL NEW ENGLAND   WINTERFARE COOKING

Salmon Croquettes

SERVES 4

2 cups cooked salmon,
    fresh or canned
1 tablespoon lemon juice
1 medium potato, peeled,
    boiled and mashed
1 onion, grated
1 egg, beaten
1 teaspoon pepper
pinch of salt
$^1/_2$ cup all-purpose flour
2 tablespoons safflower oil

Serve with:
non-fat sour cream
    blended with lemon
    juice, salt and pepper

Flake salmon apart, removing bones. In a mixing bowl, combine salmon with lemon juice, mashed potato, onion, beaten egg, spices and flour. Stir well. Form into 3-inch croquette patties, about $^1/_2$ inch thick.

Preheat frying pan. Spray with non-stick oil, then coat with safflower oil. Carefully place croquettes in hot oil. Fry until browned on both sides, then drain on paper towels. Serve hot with seasoned sour cream.

Serving: 1/4 Recipe	Calories: 363	Protein: 37 gm
Calories from Fat: 100	Total Fat: 11 gm	Dietary Fiber: 2 gm
Saturated Fat: 2 gm	Carbs: 28 gm	Sodium: 179 mg
Component of Fat: 28%	Cholesterol: 139 mg	Calcium: 120 mg

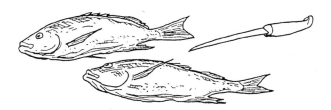

Honey-Orange Glazed Salmon

Honey-Orange Glazed Salmon is a marvelous blend of flavors.

1$^1/_2$ lbs. salmon fillets
$^1/_2$ cup orange juice
$^1/_2$ cup honey
1 teaspoon butter
1 tablespoon lemon juice
$^1/_2$ teaspoon pepper
pinch of salt

SERVES 4

Cut salmon into 4 portions. Check for bones, and remove any with pliers. Pat fish dry with paper towels.

In a small saucepan, combine remaining ingredients. Simmer sauce for 15 minutes.

Preheat broiler. Spray oven pan with non-stick oil. Place salmon on pan and coat with sauce. Slide under broiler on upper rack, leaving oven door tipped open. Baste with sauce every 5 minutes. When fillets start to brown on top, close oven door and fish will cook through in 3 minutes (do not flip fish). Spoon extra sauce over fish before serving.

Serving: 1/4 Recipe	Calories: 366	Protein: 40 gm
Calories from Fat: 63	Total Fat: 7 gm	Dietary Fiber: 0 gm
Saturated Fat: 2 gm	Carbs: 38 gm	Sodium: 142 mg
Component of Fat: 16%	Cholesterol: 115 mg	Calcium: 84 mg

Broiled Swordfish Steaks

4 swordfish steaks, sized
    to suit appetites
2 tablespoons olive oil
2 tablespoons lemon juice
1 teaspoons tamari or
    soy sauce
1 teaspoon pepper

SERVES 4

Cut off any visible fat from swordfish steaks. In a shallow pan, make a marinade of remaining ingredients. Soak swordfish steaks in marinade, spooning liquid over tops of steaks. Cover pan, and refrigerate at least 1 hour.

Preheat broiler. Spray broiler pan with non-stick oil (for easier clean-up). Place swordfish on upper rack under broiler, leaving oven door tipped open. When browned, turn steaks over, baste with marinade, and broil second side.

Serving: 1 Steak	Calories: 238	Protein: 34 gm
Calories from Fat: 92	Total Fat: 10 gm	Dietary Fiber: 0 gm
Saturated Fat: 2.5 gm	Carbs: 1 gm	Sodium: 195 mg
Component of Fat: 40%	Cholesterol: 66 mg	Calcium: 8 mg

Whale watching cruises in New England can be taken out of many ports. Humpback and finback whales are commonly seen, especially where there are banks and underwater mountain chains which breed plankton and krill for the whales to feed on. The New England whales winter and bear their young in the Caribbean, then migrate north.

COASTAL NEW ENGLAND   WINTERFARE COOKING

Cacciucco

Squid is customarily used in Cacciucco. A local fisherman claims that they are twice as sweet as lobster and only half the trouble to fix.

$\frac{1}{2}$ lb. squid or lobster
    meat
$\frac{1}{2}$ lb. shrimp, peeled and
    deveined
2 tablespoons olive oil
2 cloves garlic, minced
1 small hot red pepper
$\frac{1}{2}$ cup white wine
2 teaspoons parsley
1 tablespoon oregano
1 tablespoon grated
    lemon rind
$\frac{1}{2}$ cup Madeira
2 tablespoons tomato
    paste
$2\frac{1}{2}$ cups water
pinch of salt
1 lb. cod fillets, skinned
$\frac{1}{2}$ lb. scallops
$\frac{1}{2}$ lb. halibut
8 slices Italian bread
1 clove garlic, cut in half

SERVES 8

Clean squid: Remove the spiny portion, which looks like a translucent rod. Pull the head and legs from the envelope-like covering. If desired, remove ink sac at the base of the head. Cut squid and shrimp into small pieces.

In a deep pot, heat oil, sauté garlic and whole hot pepper. Add squid and shrimp. Cover and cook 30 minutes. Add white wine and simmer, uncovered, until it evaporates.

Mix in parsley, oregano, lemon rind, Madeira, tomato paste, water and salt. Cut cod, scallops and halibut into pieces; add to stew. Cover and simmer 15 minutes. Add water if needed, but stew must be thick.

Toast bread, rub with cut garlic and place in bowls. Remove hot red pepper, adjust seasonings, and ladle stew over toast.

Serving: 1/8 Recipe	Calories: 308	Protein: 37 gm
Calories from Fat: 59	Total Fat: 6.5 gm	Dietary Fiber: 1 gm
Saturated Fat: 1 gm	Carbs: 19 gm	Sodium: 379 mg
Component of Fat: 20%	Cholesterol: 171 mg	Calcium: 88 mg

Pasta, Beans and Grains

CONTENTS

Any Pasta, Beans and Grains recipe can be used for a
main dish or side dish by varying the amount per person.

Lobster Linguine

SERVES 4

2 tablespoons unsalted
   butter
2 cloves garlic, minced
1 teaspoon mace
1 teaspoon white pepper
1 tablespoon prepared
   sweet mustard sauce
$\frac{1}{4}$ cup clam juice
$\frac{1}{4}$ cup cognac
$\frac{1}{4}$ cup water
4 cups cooked lobster
   meat, cut into bite-
   sized pieces
1 lb. dry linguine pasta

Set a large pot of water to boil.

Heat butter in a saucepan. Add garlic and sauté until clear. Stir in mace, pepper, mustard sauce, clam juice, cognac and water. Add lobster and simmer 10 minutes.

Place pasta in boiling water, and drain when tender. With a slotted spoon, remove lobster from sauce. Toss pasta and sauce. Place pasta on dinner plates, and lobster pieces on top.

Serving: 1/4 Recipe	Calories: 564	Protein: 42 gm
Calories from Fat: 94	Total Fat: 10.5 gm	Dietary Fiber: 3 gm
Saturated Fat: 4 gm	Carbs: 67 gm	Sodium: 631 mg
Component of Fat: 16%	Cholesterol: 120 mg	Calcium: 95 mg

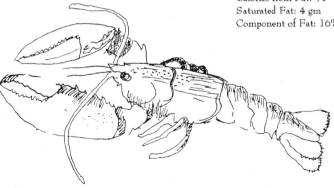

Creamy Sea Shells
with Smoked Salmon

2 cups dry small pasta
    shells
$1^1/_2$ cups canola oil
3 tablespoons flour
$1^1/_2$ cups skim milk
1 teaspoon black pepper
2 teaspoons grated onion
$^1/_2$ cup grated low-fat
    Cheddar cheese
$^1/_2$ cup non-fat sour cream
1 cup hot-smoked salmon
    (not moist "lox"
    strips) broken into
    bite-sized pieces
1 teaspoon lemon juice

SERVES 4

Boil pasta until tender. Prepare sauce while pasta is cooking.

In a small saucepan, heat oil, then blend in flour. Slowly whisk in milk, then pepper and onion. Stirring constantly, allow sauce to thicken. Turn off heat, and while stirring, gradually add grated Cheddar until it is melted. Remove from heat and fold in sour cream and smoked salmon. Mix in lemon juice.

When pasta is cooked, drain and toss with sauce. Serve at once.

Serving: 1/4 Recipe	Calories: 423	Protein: 24 gm
Calories from Fat: 87	Total Fat: 9.5 gm	Dietary Fiber: 1 gm
Saturated Fat: 2 gm	Carbs: 59 gm	Sodium: 194 mg
Component of Fat: 21%	Cholesterol: 13 mg	Calcium: 461 mg

Fisherman's Pot Pie

$2^1/_2$ cups all-purpose flour
$^1/_4$ cup safflower oil
$^1/_2$ cup ice water
2 eggs, beaten
20 small pearl onions
$^1/_2$ cup chopped celery
1 teaspoon safflower oil
3 tablespoons flour
2 teaspoons thyme
1 cup vegetable broth
1 cup skim milk blended
    with $^1/_2$ cup non-fat
    powdered milk
1 cup frozen corn kernels
1 lb. raw fish, cut into
    bite-sized pieces
1 lb. cleaned raw shellfish
    (shrimp, clams, crab...)
1 teaspoon skim milk

SERVES 8

Preheat oven to 400°. Spray a pie dish with non-stick oil.

Cut $^1/_4$ cup oil into flour with pastry cutter or knives, until mixture resembles texture of peas. Stir in ice water, then beaten eggs. Divide dough and roll between floured sheets of waxed paper to make top and bottom crusts for pie dish. Place bottom crust in pie dish.

Peel small onions and sauté with celery in 1 teaspoon safflower oil. Stir in 3 tablespoons flour and thyme. Slowly whisk in vegetable broth and milk. Cook until thickened.

Add corn, fish and shellfish. Pour into pie dish, then cover with top crust. Pinch and flute edges together. Brush top with 1 teaspoon milk and make 5 slits with knife. Bake 30 minutes.

Serving: 1/8 Recipe	Calories: 444	Protein: 42 gm
Calories from Fat: 96	Total Fat: 10.5 gm	Dietary Fiber: 2 gm
Saturated Fat: 1.5 gm	Carbs: 43 gm	Sodium: 312 mg
Component of Fat: 22%	Cholesterol: 257 mg	Calcium: 170 mg

Shells Stuffed with Crab Ricotta

SERVES 6

½ lb. large pasta shells
   for stuffing
2 teaspoons safflower oil
2 cups part-skim Ricotta
   cheese
½ cup grated low-fat
   Swiss Lorraine cheese
1 lb. fresh or canned crab
2 teaspoons garlic powder
1 teaspoon white pepper
2 tablespoons parsley
½ cup chopped onion
½ cup chopped pepper
1 clove garlic, minced
2 teaspoons olive oil
2 cups chopped peeled
   tomatoes and juice
¼ cup tomato paste
1 bay leaf
1 teaspoon oregano
salt and pepper to taste

Rapidly boil pasta shells in a large quantity of water until tender, but firm to the bite. Drain, return to pot and toss with safflower oil to keep them from sticking together.

In a mixing bowl, combine Ricotta, Swiss Lorraine, crab meat, garlic powder, white pepper and parsley. Stuff filling into shells and place in a large baking pan that's been sprayed with non-stick oil.

Sauté onion, pepper and garlic in olive oil. Add remaining ingredients and rapidly cook down until sauce has thickened. Remove bay leaf and spoon sauce over stuffed shells. Bake in 350° oven for 30 minutes.

Serving: 1/6 Recipe	Calories: 405	Protein: 32 gm
Calories from Fat: 106	Total Fat: 11.5 gm	Dietary Fiber: 3 gm
Saturated Fat: 5 gm	Carbs: 43 gm	Sodium: 384 mg
Component of Fat: 26%	Cholesterol: 73 mg	Calcium: 363 mg

Fettucine Alfredo with Baby Peas & Blackened Scallops

2 lbs. sea scallops (about $^3/_4$ inch in diameter)
3 tablespoons paprika
1 tablespoon onion powder
2 teaspoons garlic powder
2 teaspoons cumin
1 teaspoon cayenne
1 tablespoon safflower oil
2 lbs. fresh fettucine noodles
1 cup skim milk blended with $^1/_3$ cup non-fat powdered milk
1 cup fresh grated Parmesan cheese
$1^1/_2$ cups frozen baby peas
1 teaspoon black pepper

SERVES 6

Toss scallops in a colander, and lightly pat dry on a cotton towel. In a small, sturdy paper bag, combine spices. Place half of the scallops in the paper bag and shake well. Pick out scallops. Shake remaining scallops in the spice bag.

Heat a cast-iron frying pan on high heat. Briefly spray with non-stick oil, then brush with oil. Fry scallops to pan blacken on both sides.

Boil noodles in a large quantity of water until tender. Drain. Add milk and Parmesan a little at a time, tossing after each addition. Stir in scallops and peas. Heat, season with pepper.

Serving: 1/6 Recipe	Calories: 492	Protein: 44 gm
Calories from Fat: 89	Total Fat: 10 gm	Dietary Fiber: 3 gm
Saturated Fat: 3 gm	Carbs: 55 gm	Sodium: 581 mg
Component of Fat: 18%	Cholesterol: 112 mg	Calcium: 354 mg

Shrimp Creole

SERVES 4

1 tablespoon canola oil
4 tablespoons flour
1 1/2 cups vegetable
    bouillon broth
1 tablespoon canola oil
2 tablespoons dry sherry
3/4 cup chopped onion
3/4 cup chopped green
    pepper
2 cups chopped peeled
    tomatoes and juice
1 bay leaf
1 teaspoon brown sugar
1/2 teaspoon cayenne
salt and pepper to taste
1 1/2 lbs. pre-cooked and
    deveined shrimp,
    thawed and drained
4 cups cooked rice

Heat 1 tablespoon oil in a large saucepan over low heat. Make a roux by blending in flour and brown. Whisk in vegetable broth, and cook over medium-low heat.

In a separate saucepan, sauté onion and green pepper in 1 tablespoon oil and sherry until browned. Stir in chopped tomatoes and their juice, bay leaf, brown sugar, cayenne, salt and pepper. Rapidly cook down over medium-high heat until liquid is reduced by half. Stir into flour roux, cook until thickened. Add shrimp and simmer for 5 minutes.

Serve over bed of hot rice.

Serving: 1/4 Recipe	Calories: 535	Protein: 41 gm
Calories from Fat: 97	Total Fat: 11 gm	Dietary Fiber: 3 gm
Saturated Fat: 1 gm	Carbs: 64 gm	Sodium: 321 mg
Component of Fat: 18%	Cholesterol: 258 mg	Calcium: 125 mg

Rhode Island Risotto
with Parmesan Cheese

3 shallots, diced
2 tablespoons olive oil
$^{1}/_{2}$ cup grated carrot
1 clove garlic, minced
2 cups dry arborio rice
$^{1}/_{2}$ cup Marsala
6 cups vegetable broth or
    bouillon
1 cup frozen peas, thawed
$^{1}/_{2}$ cup red pepper, diced
2 canned tomatoes,
    chopped and drained
1 tablespoon butter
1 teaspoon black pepper
$^{1}/_{2}$ cup fresh grated
    Parmesan cheese

SERVES 4 (8 AS A SIDE DISH)

In a large saucepan, sauté shallots in oil. Add carrot and garlic, cook until shallots are clear. Stir in rice, then turn heat to high and add Marsala. Cook until liquid is reduced by half. Reduce heat to medium.

In a separate pot, bring vegetable broth to a boil. Add hot broth to risotto, $^{1}/_{2}$ cup at a time. Stir, and allow rice to absorb liquid after each addition. Some liquid will remain after final addition of broth. Add peas, pepper and tomato, cook 5 minutes. Add more boiling liquid if needed to make rice creamy and soft. Just before serving stir in butter, pepper and Parmesan cheese.

Serving: 1/8 Recipe	Calories: 301	Protein: 8 gm
Calories from Fat: 62	Total Fat: 7 gm	Dietary Fiber: 3 gm
Saturated Fat: 2 gm	Carbs: 49 gm	Sodium: 238 mg
Component of Fat: 21%	Cholesterol: 8 mg	Calcium: 102 mg

Wild Rice Ring with Water Chestnuts

1 cup wild rice
4 cups water
$^1/_2$ teaspoon salt
1 tablespoon canola oil
$^1/_2$ cup chopped onion
1 clove garlic, minced
$^1/_2$ cup finely chopped
    celery
$^1/_2$ cup chopped
    mushrooms
$^1/_4$ cup dry sherry
1 teaspoon nutmeg
1 small can water
    chestnuts
1 cup non-fat sour cream
1 tablespoon chopped
    parsley
salt and pepper to taste

SERVES 6

Wash wild rice several times, pouring off particles that float. Boil water and salt, then stir in rice. Cover and simmer 40 minutes or until tender. Do not stir while cooking.

Sauté onion, garlic, celery and mushrooms in oil. Turn off heat, add sherry and nutmeg. Combine with cooked rice. Press into 7-inch ring mold that has been sprayed with non-stick oil. Place ring mold in a pan of hot water in the oven. Bake at 350° for 20 minutes. Loosen edges and turn onto serving platter. Drain water chestnuts, toss with sour cream and parsley, salt and pepper to taste, and fill center of ring. Serve at once.

Serving: 1/6 Recipe   Calories: 192   Protein: 7 gm
Calories from Fat: 25   Total Fat: 3 gm   Dietary Fiber: 3 gm
Saturated Fat: .5 gm   Carbs: 32 gm   Sodium: 245 mg
Component of Fat: 13%   Cholesterol: 0 mg   Calcium: 76 mg

Hulled Barley and Sesame Seeds

1 cup whole-grain hulled
    barley
3 cups water
$^1/_4$ teaspoon salt
3 tablespoons sesame
    seeds

SERVES 4

Boil barley in salted water until tender, about $1^1/_2$ hours, adding water if necessary.

Spread sesame seeds on cookie sheet and toast in 300° oven until light brown (they burn quickly so watch carefully).

When barley has absorbed all the water and is soft, transfer to serving dish. Sprinkle toasted sesame seeds on top, and serve hot.

Serving: 1/4 Recipe	Calories: 201	Protein: 7 gm
Calories from Fat: 40	Total Fat: 4.5 gm	Dietary Fiber: 8 gm
Saturated Fat: .5 gm	Carbs: 35 gm	Sodium: 157 mg
Component of Fat: 19%	Cholesterol: 0 mg	Calcium: 85 mg

Since wheat does not grow well in New England, rye, cornmeal, barley and buckwheat are the grains and flours of traditional local cooking. Barley and winter rye grow farther north than any other food plant. The early settlers also found these grains would grow when scattered in newly cleared soil, even before tree stumps could be cleared for plowing.

Baked Beans

2 cups dried beans
    (any kind)
6 cups water
$1/3$ cup chopped onion
$1/4$ cup dark molasses
3 tablespoons ketchup
1 cup chopped canned
    tomatoes and juice
2 tablespoons canola oil
1 cup beer
1 teaspoon curry powder
1 tablespoon
    Worcestershire sauce

SERVES 6

Wash beans. Put in pot with water and bring to a full boil. Simmer 30 minutes, then remove from heat. Let sit 1 hour, then return to heat and simmer 1 hour, or until tender. Mix in all other ingredients.

Tranfer into covered bean pot.   Bake in 250° oven 6 to 7 hours, adding water if necessary.

Serving: 1/6 Recipe	Calories: 324	Protein: 16 gm
Calories from Fat: 49	Total Fat: 5.5 gm	Dietary Fiber: 11 gm
Saturated Fat: .5 gm	Carbs: 53 gm	Sodium: 106 mg
Component of Fat: 15%	Cholesterol: 0 mg	Calcium: 274 mg

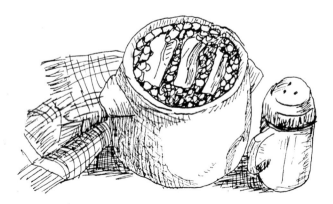

Hopping John

Eat Hopping John on New Year's Day and you'll have good luck all year.

2 cups dried black-eyed
   peas
6 cups soup broth, any
   kind
2 cups chopped onions
1 teaspoon black pepper
1 teaspoon cayenne
2 cloves garlic, minced
3 bay leaves

Serve with:
8 cups boiled rice

SERVES 8

Wash dried black-eyed peas, then bring to a boil in broth. Simmer 5 mintues, then remove from heat and let stand 1 hour.

Add remaining ingredients to pot, and bring back to a boil. Simmer 2 hours. Remove bay leaves and slightly mash mixture.

Serve over hot boiled rice.

Serving: 1/8 Recipe	Calories: 284	Protein: 7 gm
Calories from Fat: 7	Total Fat: .5 gm	Dietary Fiber: 4 gm
Saturated Fat: 0 gm	Carbs: 62 gm	Sodium: 70 mg
Component of Fat: 2%	Cholesterol: 0 mg	Calcium: 97 mg

Succotash

2 cups cooked lima beans
2 cups cooked corn
    (fresh or frozen)
2 teaspoons butter
1/2 teaspoon salt
1 teaspoon pepper
1 teaspoon paprika

Garnish:
parsley

SERVES 6

Boil water in bottom pan of double boiler. In the top pan, combine all ingredients. Cover and cook 30 minutes over boiling water.

Transfer to serving bowl and sprinkle with chopped parsley.

Serving: 1/6 Recipe	Calories: 127	Protein: 5 gm
Calories from Fat: 16	Total Fat: 2 gm	Dietary Fiber: 4 gm
Saturated Fat: 1 gm	Carbs: 25 gm	Sodium: 220 mg
Component of Fat: 12%	Cholesterol: 4 mg	Calcium: 23 mg

During the eighteenth century Indian corn was the most important crop, and the food staple of settlers and Indians. The Indians had taught the settlers to plant corn "when the oakleaf is as big as a mouse's ear." The native women instructed them to poke a hole in the ground and drop in 4 or 5 corn kernels, with part of a dead fish for fertilizer.

Vegetables
and
Sauces

CONTENTS

Carrot Tzimmes

3 tablespoons barley
1 cup water
5 cups carrots, peeled and
     cut into 1-inch rounds
1 cup grated apple
pinch of salt
2 tablespoons honey
$1/2$ cup water
$1^1/_2$ tablespoons butter
$1/2$ teaspoon powdered
     ginger

SERVES 6

Bring barley and water to a boil in a covered pot. Turn off heat, let set 1 hour, then drain.

Add remaining ingredients, including $1/2$ cup of water, to the pot. Place on low heat, cover, and cook at least 1 hour, until barley is tender. Stir occasionally, and add more water if tzimmes dries out.

Serving: 1/6 Recipe	Calories: 143	Protein: 2 gm
Calories from Fat: 32	Total Fat: 3.5 gm	Dietary Fiber: 6 gm
Saturated Fat: 2 gm	Carbs: 28 gm	Sodium: 138 mg
Component of Fat: 21%	Cholesterol: 8 mg	Calcium: 46 mg

Corn Fritters

SERVES 4

2 cups frozen corn kernels
2 eggs, separated
1 cup skim milk
$\frac{1}{2}$ teaspoon baking soda
1 cup all-purpose flour
1 tablespoon safflower oil
    for frying

Defrost frozen corn and drain. In a large mixing bowl, mash corn with potato masher or pastry cutter. Mix in egg yolks and milk.

Combine baking soda and flour. Stir into corn mixture. In a separate bowl, whip egg whites until stiff, then fold into batter.

Spray frying pan with non-stick oil, lightly coat with safflower oil. Heat over medium burner. When oil is hot,   drop batter by heaping tablespoon, frying until golden on both sides.

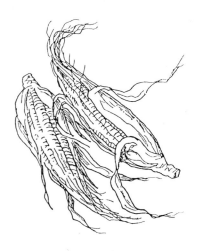

Serving: 1/4 Recipe
Calories from Fat: 57
Saturated Fat: 1 gm
Component of Fat: 21%

Calories: 260
Total Fat: 6.5 gm
Carbs: 42 gm
Cholesterol: 107 mg

Protein: 11 gm
Dietary Fiber: 3 gm
Sodium: 225 mg
Calcium: 94 mg

Refreshed Winter Peas

This simple recipe puts a fresh taste back into frozen peas.

1 lb. frozen peas
2 teaspoons butter
2 tablespoons vegetable
    broth
1/4 cup finely chopped
    onion
1 teaspoon chopped mint
salt and pepper to taste

SERVES 6

Warm peas, just until tender. Drain.

While peas are heating, melt butter with bouillon, and sauté onion until clear. Pour over drained peas, add mint, salt and pepper. Toss lightly, serve hot.

Serving: 1/6 Recipe	Calories: 75	Protein: 4 gm
Calories from Fat: 14	Total Fat: 1.5 gm	Dietary Fiber: 4 gm
Saturated Fat: 1 gm	Carbs: 12 gm	Sodium: 101 mg
Component of Fat: 18%	Cholesterol: 4 mg	Calcium: 22 mg

The simple pea is an excellent year-round food. The fresh tender peas of spring are sweet and crunchy right off the vine. Dried peas have provided winter nourishment for thousands of years. Peas can also be preserved by canning, freezing and pickling. They contain protein, carbohydrates, Vitamins A, B complex and C, iron and calcium.

Green Beans Amandine

SERVES 4

1 lb. frozen green beans
1 teaspoon butter
2 tablespoons white wine
3 tablespoons sliced
    almonds
pinch of salt
$\frac{1}{2}$ teaspoon pepper

Warm green beans in covered pot until tender, but not limp. Drain and return to pot.

While green beans are cooking, toast sliced almonds on baking sheet in 300° oven, then sauté in butter and wine. Pour over drained green beans. Add salt and pepper, toss to coat. Serve hot.

Serving: 1/4 Recipe
Calories from Fat: 41
Saturated Fat: 1 gm
Component of Fat: 42%

Calories: 89
Total Fat: 4.5 gm
Carbs: 9 gm
Cholesterol: 3 mg

Protein: 3 gm
Dietary Fiber: 4 gm
Sodium: 51 mg
Calcium: 75 mg

Gosport Church
Star Island, Isles of Shoals

Honey-Glazed Turnips

4 cups whole turnips
1 teaspoon butter
1 tablespoon safflower oil
2 tablespoons honey
2 teaspoons lemon juice
salt and pepper to taste

SERVES 4

Peel turnips and cut into quarters. Simmer in boiling water 30 minutes, or until tender. Drain, and place in serving bowl.

While turnips are cooking, melt butter with oil in a small saucepan. Add honey, lemon juice, salt and pepper, and warm over low heat. Pour sauce over turnips in serving bowl.

Serving: 1/4 Recipe	Calories: 77	Protein: 1 gm
Calories from Fat: 40	Total Fat: 4.5 gm	Dietary Fiber: 3 gm
Saturated Fat: 1.5 gm	Carbs: 11 gm	Sodium: 128 mg
Component of Fat: 46%	Cholesterol: 5 mg	Calcium: 35 mg

Sherried Mushrooms Au Gratin

1 lb. mushrooms
1 small onion
4 whole cloves
1 small bay leaf
1 tablespoon olive oil
1½ tablespoons flour
1¼ cups skim milk
pinch of salt
pinch of pepper
pinch of nutmeg
3 tablespoons dry sherry
2 teaspoons grated
    Parmesan cheese

Optional:
15 shucked oysters

SERVES 5

Cut large mushrooms in quarters and small mushrooms in half. Chop onion and tie in cheesecloth with cloves and bay leaf to make spice bag.

In a saucepan over low heat, warm olive oil, then blend in flour. With a whisk, blend in milk, salt, pepper and nutmeg until smooth. Place spice bag in sauce. Cook on low heat 15 minutes, stirring frequently. When thickened, remove spice bag, stir in sherry.

Preheat oven to 375°. Spray oven dish with non-stick oil. Place mushrooms, and oysters if desired, in dish. Cover with sauce, then sprinkle with Parmesan. Bake 25 minutes, or until nicely browned on top.

Serving: 1/5 Recipe	Calories: 110	Protein: 5 gm
Calories from Fat: 32	Total Fat: 3.5 gm	Dietary Fiber: 2 gm
Saturated Fat: .5 gm	Carbs: 12 gm	Sodium: 73 mg
Component of Fat: 27%	Cholesterol: 2 mg	Calcium: 97 mg

Broccoli Dijonnaise

Dijonnaise is a wonderful sauce that can be poured over most steamed vegetables. This recipe makes 2 cups of Dijonnaise.

1 large head broccoli

SERVES 5

Dijonnaise Sauce:
2 tablespoons canola oil
$\frac{1}{3}$ cup chopped onion
$\frac{1}{4}$ teaspoon thyme
$\frac{1}{4}$ teaspoon garlic powder
$\frac{1}{2}$ bay leaf
1 cup vegetable broth
1 cup chopped and peeled
    tomatoes
2 tablespoons flour
1 cup skim milk
$\frac{1}{4}$ teaspoon nutmeg
1 tablespoon Dijon
    mustard
2 tablespoons Madeira
salt and pepper to taste

Divide broccoli into large florets. Just before Dijonnaise is ready, steam broccoli about 7 minutes, until it has just turned tender.

Sauté onion in 1 tablespoon oil until clear. Add spices. Mix in broth (can be made from bouillon cube). Chop tomatoes into small pieces, drain and add to broth. Simmer until liquid is reduced by half. Remove bay leaf.

In a separate saucepan, heat remaining tablespoon of oil, blend in flour, then whisk in milk and nutmeg. Blend and cook until thick and smooth. Combine both sauces, stir in Dijon mustard, Madeira, salt and pepper.

Serving: 1/5 Recipe	Calories: 133	Protein: 5 gm
Calories from Fat: 58	Total Fat: 6.5 gm	Dietary Fiber: 3 gm
Saturated Fat: .5 gm	Carbs: 13 gm	Sodium: 83 mg
Component of Fat: 40%	Cholesterol: 1 mg	Calcium: 110 mg

Curry Creamed Cauliflower and Peas

1 head cooked cauliflower
   (2$\frac{1}{2}$ cups florets)
2 cups frozen peas
1$\frac{1}{2}$ tablespoons canola oil
2 tablespoons wheat flour
2 teaspoons curry
1 teaspoon turmeric
$\frac{1}{2}$ teaspoon ground
   cardamom
1 cup skim milk
1 tablespoon chopped
   parsley
pinch of salt
pinch of paprika

SERVES 6

Set cauliflower and peas over low heat to warm. Do not overcook.

Heat oil in a large saucepan. Blend in flour and seasonings to make a roux. Use a whisk to blend in milk. Stir until sauce is smooth and thick. Drain vegetables, add to sauce and heat together. Place in serving bowl, and sprinkle with parsley, salt and paprika.

Serving: 1/6 Recipe	Calories: 111	Protein: 6 gm
Calories from Fat: 37	Total Fat: 4 gm	Dietary Fiber: 5 gm
Saturated Fat: .5 gm	Carbs: 14 gm	Sodium: 96 mg
Component of Fat: 32%	Cholesterol: 1 mg	Calcium: 81 mg

New Potatoes

1¹/₂ lbs. small red
   potatoes
1¹/₂ tablespoons butter
1¹/₂ tablespoons olive oil
¹/₃ cup finely chopped
   scallions
1 teaspoon crushed garlic
2 teaspoons lemon juice
1 teaspoon dill
pinch of salt
pinch of pepper

SERVES 6

Scrub potatoes and place in a large pot of boiling water. Simmer for 20-25 minutes, until potatoes are tender but not mushy.

While potatoes are cooking, melt butter with olive oil. Briefly sauté scallions and garlic, then add lemon juice and spices. Drain potatoes and place in serving bowl. Pour sauce over potatoes, and toss to coat.

Serving: 1/6 Recipe	Calories: 159	Protein: 2 gm
Calories from Fat: 60	Total Fat: 6.5 gm	Dietary Fiber: 2 gm
Saturated Fat: 2.5 gm	Carbs: 24 gm	Sodium: 57 mg
Component of Fat: 36%	Cholesterol: 8 mg	Calcium: 23 mg

Rhode Island calls itself "The Ocean State." By navigating the deep waters of Narragansett Bay, a large ship can sail two-thirds of the way through the state. Providence is at the head of the bay, and Newport on an island at its mouth. In Colonial times, these cities were maritime trade centers for fish, lumber, shipbuilding, rum, and even ponies.

COASTAL NEW ENGLAND   WINTERFARE COOKING

Candied Cranberry Sweet Potatoes

4 medium-sized sweet
   potatoes
1 cup fresh cranberries
$^1/_2$ cup apple juice or cider
$^3/_4$ cup brown sugar
3 tablespoons lemon juice
$^1/_3$ cup honey
1 tablespoon melted
   butter

SERVES 4

Cut sweet potatoes in half and boil in water until tender. Cool in cold water, then peel off skins. Place sweet potatoes in a baking dish that's been sprayed with non-stick oil.

In a saucepan, combine cranberries, apple juice or cider and brown sugar. Cook about 25 minutes. Mix in lemon juice and spoon cranberry sauce over sweet potatoes. Combine honey with melted butter and pour on top. Bake in preheated 325° oven 20 minutes.

Serving: 1/4 Recipe
Calories from Fat: 34
Saturated Fat: 2 gm
Component of Fat: 6%

Calories: 559
Total Fat: 4 gm
Carbs: 123 gm
Cholesterol: 8 mg

Protein: 13 gm
Dietary Fiber: 16 gm
Sodium: 63 mg
Calcium: 134 mg

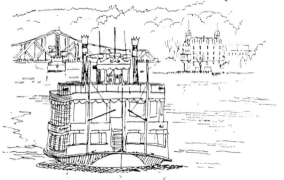

The riverboat *Becky Thatcher* on the Connecticut River by the Goodspeed Opera House. Haddam, Connecticut

Grilled Eggplant Italiano

Filling:

$^1/_2$ cup grated part-skim
    mozzarella cheese

3 tablespoons grated
    Parmesan cheese

$^3/_4$ cup part-skim Ricotta
    cheese

1 egg

1 teaspoon oregano

1 tablespoon parsley

basil and pepper to taste

Batter:

1 egg

3 tablespoons flour

$^2/_3$ cup skim milk

1 tablespoon canola oil

2 large eggplants

2 tablespoons canola oil

flour for dipping

$1^1/_2$ cups spiced tomato
    sauce

SERVES 8

Blend together filling ingredients until smooth. Cover and chill.

Beat batter ingredients together until smooth.

Peel eggplant. Cut lengthwise into thin slices. Spray a large griddle with non-stick oil, then coat with canola. Preheat on medium-high. Dip eggplant slices in flour, then in batter. Fry in griddle until lightly browned on both sides. Drain on paper towels.

While eggplant is still warm, spoon 2 tablespoons filling mixture across eggplant, near the wider end. Roll up loosely, jelly-roll style. Place in baking dish that's been sprayed with non-stick oil. Cover with tomato sauce. Bake in preheated 375° oven for 15 minutes.

Serving: 1/8 Recipe	Calories: 212	Protein: 11 gm
Calories from Fat: 95	Total Fat: 10.5 gm	Dietary Fiber: 4 gm
Saturated Fat: 3 gm	Carbs: 20 gm	Sodium: 425 mg
Component of Fat: 43%	Cholesterol: 66 mg	Calcium: 207 mg

Spinach-Ricotta Dumplings

1 lb. frozen, chopped
    spinach
1 1/2 cups part-skim
    Ricotta cheese
1 cup bread crumbs
2 eggs, beaten
1 clove garlic, minced
1 small onion, grated
1/4 cup grated Parmesan
    cheese
1 teaspoon basil
salt and pepper to taste
1 cup wheat or rye flour
2 quarts salt-water

Serve with:
mustard sauce

SERVES 8

Rinse and squeeze moisture from defrosted spinach leaves. Mix spinach with Ricotta, bread crumbs, eggs, garlic, onion, Parmesan, basil, salt and pepper. Roll into 1-inch balls, then roll balls lightly in flour. Chill in refrigerator.

Bring 2 quarts of salt-water to a boil in a deep saucepan. Turn heat to medium-high. Drop spinach-ricotta balls into simmering water. In 4-5 minutes the balls will rise to the surface, indicating they are finished cooking. Remove with a slotted spoon. Serve on toothpicks with your favorite mustard sauce.

Serving: 1/8 Recipe	Calories: 180	Protein: 12 gm
Calories from Fat: 57	Total Fat: 6.5 gm	Dietary Fiber: 4 gm
Saturated Fat: 3.5 gm	Carbs: 20 gm	Sodium: 228 mg
Component of Fat: 30%	Cholesterol: 69 mg	Calcium: 267 mg

Butternut Casserole

SERVES 8

6 cups fresh butternut
    squash, peeled and
    cut in $^1/_2$-inch cubes
$^1/_2$ cup chopped onion
1 cup shredded carrots
1 cup chopped celery
2 tablespoons canola oil
$1^1/_2$ cups bread crumbs
1 teaspoon basil
1 teaspoon thyme
salt and pepper to taste
2 cups non-fat plain
    yogurt
$^1/_2$ cup low-fat Cheddar
1 egg, beaten
$^1/_4$ cup chopped chives
2 tablespoons toasted
    sesame seeds

Preheat oven to 350°. Spray a 2-quart casserole with non-stick oil.

Steam squash until tender. Sauté onion, carrots and celery in canola oil. Remove from heat and stir in bread crumbs, basil, thyme, salt and pepper. Place half of the squash in the casserole, cover with stuffing, and then the other half of the squash.

In a saucepan, combine yogurt and cheese over low heat until cheese melts. Remove from heat and whisk in the beaten egg and chives. Pour over squash, then sprinkle sesame seeds over top. Bake 30 minutes.

Serving: 1/8 Recipe	Calories: 205	Protein: 12 gm
Calories from Fat: 51	Total Fat: 5.5 gm	Dietary Fiber: 7 gm
Saturated Fat: 1 gm	Carbs: 29 gm	Sodium: 148 mg
Component of Fat: 23%	Cholesterol: 31 mg	Calcium: 369 mg

Orange Maple Acorn Squash

SERVES 4

2 medium-sized acorn
   squash
8 tablespoons maple syrup
4 tablespoons orange juice
   concentrate
2 teaspoons cinnamon
2 teaspoons butter
4 pinches of salt
boiling water

Preheat oven to 375°. Cut squash lengthwise to show shape. Scoop out seeds and stringy fibers. Place snugly in deep baking dish, open side up. Fill center of each squash half with 2 tablespoons maple syrup, 1 tablespoon orange juice concentrate, $1/2$ teaspoon cinnamon, $1/2$ teaspoon butter and a pinch of salt. Place baking dish on oven rack, then carefully pour 1 inch of boiling water in pan to surround squash. Bake 40 minutes, or until tender and golden.

Serving: 1/2 Squash	Calories: 278	Protein: 3 gm
Calories from Fat: 22	Total Fat: 2.5 gm	Dietary Fiber: 10 gm
Saturated Fat: 1.5 gm	Carbs: 67 gm	Sodium: 150 mg
Component of Fat: 7%	Cholesterol: 5 mg	Calcium: 154 mg

Orange Cranberry Sauce

MAKES $2^1/_2$ CUPS

1 lb. fresh cranberries
1 cup orange juice
$1^1/_2$ cups brown sugar
1 teaspoon cinnamon

Wash cranberries. Cook in orange juice until their skins burst, then cook 5 minutes more. Stir in sugar and cinnamon. Serve warm, or chill to firm and use as a relish.

Serving: 1/4 Cup	Calories: 288	Protein: 11 gm
Calories from Fat: 6	Total Fat: .5 gm	Dietary Fiber: 11 gm
Saturated Fat: 0 gm	Carbs: 62 gm	Sodium: 16 mg
Component of Fat: 2%	Cholesterol: 0 mg	Calcium: 91 mg

Sesame Brussels Sprouts

1 lb. Brussels sprouts
$^1/_2$ cup crushed crumbs
    from rye crackers
2 tablespoons sesame
    seeds
2 tablespoons grated
    Parmesan cheese

Optional:
$^1/_2$ cup roasted and
    chopped chestnuts

SERVES 4

Steam Brussels sprouts until tender. Briefly toast crumbs and sesame seeds on a cookie sheet until golden.

Drain Brussels sprouts. Combine with cheese, and if desired, chestnuts. Transfer into casserole sprayed with non-stick oil. Sprinkle top with toasted crumbs and sesame seeds. Bake in 350° oven 15 minutes.

Serving: 1/4 Recipe	Calories: 181	Protein: 8 gm
Calories from Fat: 32	Total Fat: 3.5 gm	Dietary Fiber: 12 gm
Saturated Fat: 1 gm	Carbs: 34 gm	Sodium: 300 mg
Component of Fat: 16%	Cholesterol: 2 mg	Calcium: 137 mg

By 1860 most American homes had an iron cooking range instead of a searing open hearth fire. Besides ease of use and overall convenience, precision of heat became a possibility. In 1880 gas was widely available, and these stoves replaced the solid-fuel models. Electric "hot plate" stoves hit the market in 1890, but were not popular until the 1920's.

Braised Leeks

4 leeks
2 tablespoons lemon juice
$^1/_2$ cup vegetable broth
1 teaspoon sugar
1 teaspoon white pepper
1 teaspoon butter

SERVES 4

Remove and discard upper leaves and tough outer green stalks from leeks. Wash leeks well, then slice in half lengthwise. Spray stove-top skillet or casserole with non-stick oil. Arrange leeks in skillet.

In a small mixing bowl, combine remaining ingredients, then pour over leeks. Bring to a boil over medium-high heat. Cover and reduce heat to low. Simmer until tender.

Serving: 1/4 Recipe	Calories: 97	Protein: 2 gm
Calories from Fat: 13	Total Fat: 1.5 gm	Dietary Fiber: 2 gm
Saturated Fat: .5 gm	Carbs: 21 gm	Sodium: 46 mg
Component of Fat: 12%	Cholesterol: 3 mg	Calcium: 76 mg

Desserts
and
Sweets

CONTENTS

Note: The nutritional analysis for pies is based on 8 pieces per pie.

Cherry Tarts

Tart Shells:
1 cup all-purpose flour
2 tablespoons sugar
3 tablespoons canola oil
1 egg yolk
$\frac{1}{2}$ teaspoon vanilla
1 tablespoon lemon juice
2 tablespoons powdered
   sugar

Cherry Tart Filling:
$\frac{1}{2}$ cup apple juice
2 tablespoons quick-
   cooking tapioca
1 tablespoon butter
$\frac{1}{3}$ cup sugar (more if
   cherries are bitter)
$\frac{1}{2}$ cup brown sugar
2 teaspoons lemon juice
4 cups unsweetened fresh,
   canned or frozen
   pitted cherries

MAKES SIX 3-INCH TARTS

Tart Shells: Combine flour and sugar. Using a pastry cutter or fingertips, work canola oil into flour. Make well in center, add egg yolk, vanilla and lemon juice. Mix with fingers until dough forms a ball and is not sticky. Cover and chill 30 minutes. Roll dough between sheets of wax paper to $\frac{1}{8}$-inch thickness. Cut out tarts to line pans. Dough can also be cut to fit tins for large muffins, with sides of tart $1\frac{1}{2}$-inches high. Bake in 400° oven 7 minutes. Unmold shells, cool on wire rack. Dust with powdered sugar.

Filling: Mix apple juice and tapioca in a small bowl. Combine butter, sugars, lemon juice and cherries in a saucepan, cook 10 minutes over medium-low heat. Add tapioca mixture and bring to a boil. Cool at room temperature 10 minutes, then pour into shells.

Serving: 1 Tart	Calories: 395	Protein: 4 gm
Calories from Fat: 93	Total Fat: 10.5 gm	Dietary Fiber: 3 gm
Saturated Fat: 2 gm	Carbs: 75 gm	Sodium: 32 mg
Component of Fat: 22%	Cholesterol: 41 mg	Calcium: 49 mg

Holiday Strudel

*My grandmother created this recipe more than 60 years ago. Since then,
it has been present (but not for long) at all major family celebrations.*

Filling:
1 large lemon
2 cups golden raisins
1 cup chopped pecans
1 lb. each unsweetened
     pineapple, peach,
     apricot and orange
     marmalade preserves
$^1/_2$ cup shredded coconut
2 tablespoons quick
     tapioca
$^1/_2$ cup plain breadcrumbs

Pastry Dough:
2 cups flour
$^1/_8$ teaspoon baking soda
2 tablespoons sugar
2 eggs
$^1/_4$ cup canola oil
$^1/_2$ teaspoon vinegar
$1^1/_2$ tablespoons water
brushing/tops: canola oil,
     cinnamon, sugar

MAKES 100 PIECES

In a large bowl, squeeze juice from lemon and
grate rind into bowl. Add remaining filling
ingredients. Mix, cover and chill 24 hours.

Process pastry dough ingredients in a mixer,
then cover to prevent drying out. On a floured
cloth, roll a 2-inch ball of dough into a 12" x 8"
rectangle. Lightly brush with oil. Place $1^1/_2$
inch wide by $^3/_4$ inch high strip of filling along a
12-inch edge. Use the cloth to raise the edge
and roll up the strudel. Pinch ends, and
transfer to cookie sheet sprayed with non-stick
oil. Place rolls 2 inches apart on cookie sheet.
Brush with oil, sprinkle with cinnamon and
sugar. With a sharp knife (starting $^1/_2$ inch
from ends) slice top of roll at 1-inch intervals.
Bake in 350° oven for 25 minutes. Cool on
pan 10 minutes, then on brown paper. Cut into
pieces at slice marks, and separate to cool.

Serving: 1 Piece	Calories: 63	Protein: 1 gm
Calories from Fat: 16	Total Fat: 1.5 gm	Dietary Fiber: 1 gm
Saturated Fat: .5 gm	Carbs: 12 gm	Sodium: 26 mg
Component of Fat: 24%	Cholesterol: 4 mg	Calcium: 9 mg

Maple Apple Pie

MAKES ONE 9-INCH PIE

$2^2/_3$ cups all-purpose
    flour
4 tablespoons sugar
$^1/_4$ teaspoon salt
$^1/_4$ cup canola oil
$^1/_2$ cup cold skim milk
6 cups apples, peeled
    and sliced
1 tablespoon lemon juice
$^1/_2$ cup maple syrup
$^1/_2$ cup brown sugar
$^1/_2$ teaspoon vanilla
    extract
2 tablespoons cornstarch
4 tablespoons apple juice
1 tablespoon butter
1 tablespoon sugar
1 teaspoon cinnamon

NOTE: Hot pie is best
after cooling 20 minutes.

Sift flour, sugar and salt together. In a separate bowl, combine oil and milk. Pour into flour, then blend with a fork and roll into a ball. If too dry to hold together, add a little milk. Wrap in plastic and chill 15 minutes. Divide dough into 2 pieces. Roll each piece between sheets of wax paper. Place one in pie dish sprayed with non-stick oil. After crust is filled, place the other piece on top, pinch edges together, flute and trim.

Preheat oven to 400°. Mix apples, lemon juice, maple syrup, brown sugar and vanilla. Dissolve cornstarch in apple juice, stir into apples. Rest 15 minutes then stir again. Pour into crust, spread evenly and dot with butter. Place top crust on pie as stated above. Make five slits in top crust. Sprinkle with cinnamon and sugar. Bake about 40 minutes.

Serving: 1 Piece	Calories: 417	Protein: 5 gm
Calories from Fat: 83	Total Fat: 9 gm	Dietary Fiber: 3 gm
Saturated Fat: 1.5 gm	Carbs: 81 gm	Sodium: 105 mg
Component of Fat: 19%	Cholesterol: 4 mg	Calcium: 71 mg

COASTAL NEW ENGLAND   WINTERFARE COOKING

Persimmon Pumpkin Pie

Here's an interesting recipe for the beautiful persimmon. Early colonists' winter meals frequently included pumpkin and persimmon.

1$\frac{1}{2}$ cups all-purpose flour
2 tablespoons sugar
$\frac{1}{4}$ cup canola oil
5 tablespoons ice water
1 tablespoon skim milk
1 native persimmon
    (non-Japanese variety)
2 cups cooked or canned
    mashed pumpkin
1 cup skimmed
    evaporated milk
$\frac{1}{3}$ cup molasses
1$\frac{1}{2}$ cups brown sugar
3 eggs, slightly beaten
1 teaspoon baking powder
2 teaspoons cinnamon
1 teaspoon nutmeg

MAKES 1 PIE

Combine flour and sugar in mixing bowl. Using pastry cutter or two knives, cut in oil until consistancy of peas. Mix in water and milk. Cover with plastic, chill in refrigerator 15 minutes. Spray large pie plate with non-stick oil. Roll dough between layers of waxed paper. Place in pie plate, flute and trim edges. Lightly spray shell with vegetable oil.

Steam whole persimmon 25 minutes, then cool, cut and press through strainer. Mix persimmon pulp with remaining ingredients, beat well. Pour into pie shell. Bake in preheated 400° oven for 15 minutes, reduce heat to 350° and bake 35 minutes more.

Serving: 1 Piece	Calories: 407	Protein: 7 gm
Calories from Fat: 84	Total Fat: 9.5 gm	Dietary Fiber: 1 gm
Saturated Fat: 1 gm	Carbs: 76 gm	Sodium: 133 mg
Component of Fat: 20%	Cholesterol: 81 mg	Calcium: 207 mg

The North American persimmon was introduced to the early settlers by the Indian women. Though at first thought inedible, the Indians told the newcomers not to harvest the fruit until after the first frost when the persimmon loses its astringency. Persimmons were used in preserves, dried, and reduced to flour for breads and puddings.

COASTAL NEW ENGLAND   WINTERFARE COOKING

Cranberry Walnut Ring

SERVES 10

2 cups cranberries
2 cups sugar
1 tablespoon finely grated
   orange rind
2 tablespoons softened butter
2 tablespoons safflower oil
2 teaspoons vanilla
1 egg
2 cups all-purpose flour
2 teaspoons baking powder
1 teaspoon baking soda
$\frac{1}{2}$ teaspoon nutmeg
1 teaspoon cinnamon
1 cup skim milk
$\frac{1}{2}$ cup chopped walnuts

Preheat oven to 350°. Process cranberries with sugar in food processor until coarsely chopped. Transfer cranberries to saucepan and cook 5 minutes over low heat, stirring constantly. Remove from heat and add orange rind.

In a medium mixing bowl, cream together butter, oil, vanilla and egg. Mix in sugared cranberries. In a separate bowl, sift together flour, baking powder, baking soda, nutmeg and cinnamon. Alternately stir in flour mixture and milk to the creamed cranberry mixture. Fold in chopped walnuts.

Spray a Bundt pan with non-stick oil. Pour batter into pan and bake 40-45 minutes, or until a toothpick inserted in center of cake comes out clean. Remove from oven and cool 10 minutes in pan before turning out onto wire rack to cool.

Serving: 1/10 Recipe	Calories: 474	Protein: 14 gm
Calories from Fat: 90	Total Fat: 10 gm	Dietary Fiber: 11 gm
Saturated Fat: 2 gm	Carbs: 84 gm	Sodium: 59 mg
Component of Fat: 19%	Cholesterol: 28 mg	Calcium: 95 mg

Pear Compote

4 fresh pears

$^1/_4$ cup sugar

1 tablespoon finely grated
lemon zest

1 tablespoon fresh lemon
juice

$^1/_4$ teaspoon powdered
ginger

SERVES 4

Peel, core and cut pears into large pieces. In a large saucepan whisk together sugar, lemon zest, lemon juice and ginger. Add pears.

Cook over medium-low heat 3 minutes, stirring constantly. When pears start to juice-up, raise heat and gently simmer 8 minutes, stirring occasionally.

Serve immediately, or store in refrigerator in covered container.

Serving: 1/4 Recipe
Calories from Fat: 6
Saturated Fat: 0 gm
Component of Fat: 3%

Calories: 149
Total Fat: .5 gm
Carbs: 38 gm
Cholesterol: 0 mg

Protein: 1 gm
Dietary Fiber: 4 gm
Sodium: 0 mg
Calcium: 21 mg

Boston Cream Pie

SERVES 8

Cake Batter:
$^{1}/_{4}$ cup safflower oil
$2^{1}/_{2}$ cups sifted cake flour
1 teaspoon baking powder
$^{1}/_{2}$ teaspoon salt
$1^{1}/_{2}$ cups sugar
$1^{1}/_{4}$ cups skim milk
2 teaspoons vanilla
2 eggs

Cream Filling:
$^{1}/_{2}$ cup sugar
1 tablespoon cornstarch
$1^{1}/_{2}$ cups skim milk
2 egg yolks
1 teaspoon vanilla extract

Topping:
$^{1}/_{2}$ cup powdered sugar

Cakes: Preheat oven to 350°. Spray two 9-inch round layer cake pans with non-stick oil. In a large mixing bowl, use electric beaters to blend cake batter ingredients. Beat 3 minutes on high speed. Pour into two 9-inch round baking pans. Bake 30 minutes, or until toothpick inserted in cakes comes out clean. Cool in cake pans for 10 minutes, then turn onto wire rack and cool thoroughly.

Cream Filling: In a saucepan, mix sugar, cornstarch, milk and egg yolks. Stirring constantly, cook over medium heat until mixture boils for one minute. Remove from heat and stir in vanilla. Cool to room temperature before layering.

Spread cream filling between layers and sprinkle top of Boston Cream Pie with powdered sugar.

Serving: 1 Piece	Calories: 486	Protein: 9 gm
Calories from Fat: 88	Total Fat: 10 gm	Dietary Fiber: 1 gm
Saturated Fat: 1.5 gm	Carbs: 91 gm	Sodium: 257 mg
Component of Fat: 18%	Cholesterol: 108 mg	Calcium: 142 mg

Plum Sorbet

2 cups plums, fresh
   frozen, or canned
$^1/_2$ cup apple juice
$^1/_4$-$^1/_2$ cup sugar,
   depending on
   sweetness of plums
lemon wedges

SERVES 4

Process plums in blender. In a fine sieve, strain skin pieces from purée.

Combine apple juice with sugar in a saucepan. Stir over low heat until sugar is dissolved. Remove from heat and mix in plum purée.

Pour into 8-inch square pan and place in freezer. Using spatula, stir every 15 minutes until creamy, about 2 hours, then cover and allow to freeze.   To serve, scoop into small dishes and garnish with lemon wedges.

Serving: 1/4 Recipe	Calories: 159	Protein: 1 gm
Calories from Fat: 8	Total Fat: 1 gm	Dietary Fiber: 2 gm
Saturated Fat: 0 gm	Carbs: 29 gm	Sodium: 1 mg
Component of Fat: 5%	Cholesterol: 0 mg	Calcium: 8 mg

In 1845 John Brundy Brown opened the Portland Sugar House utilizing a new process converting molasses into a high grade of "white" sugar. He produced 250 barrels a day and grossed over $1,500,000 a year. To supply the Sugar House, Mr. Brown kept a fleet of brigs and schooners sailing from Matanzas and Cardenas to Portland, Maine.

Blueberry Tea Cake with Honey

SERVES 12

2 cups all-purpose flour
4 tablespoons cornmeal
2 teaspoons baking
    powder
1 teaspoon baking soda
$1/_4$ cup brown sugar
1 teaspoon nutmeg,
    cinnamon or cloves
2 tablespoons melted
    butter
1 egg
1 cup honey
1 cup low-fat buttermilk
1 teaspoon vanilla extract
2 cups blueberries, tossed
    in 2 tablespoons flour

Glaze:
1 cup powdered sugar
1 teaspoon almond
    extract
2+ tablespoons skim milk

Preheat oven to 350°. Spray 9" x 5" loaf pan, 7" x 11" cake pan, or three 6-ounce metal juice cans with non-stick vegetable oil.

In a large mixing bowl, combine all dry ingredients. In a separate bowl, beat together liquid ingredients until creamy. Whip liquid mixture into dry ingredients. Lightly fold flour-coated blueberries into batter. Pour batter into prepared baking pan or divide equally between metal cans. Bake loaf or cake pan 40-45 minutes, or tea-loafs in metal cans about 30 minutes. Allow to cool 10 minutes in pan or cans before removing.

Combine all ingredients for glaze, using just enough milk to make glaze drizzle over cake. While cake is still warm, drizzle glaze over top and down sides. Best if served while still warm, or within 24 hours of baking.

Serving: 1/12 Cake	Calories: 280	Protein: 12 gm
Calories from Fat: 36	Total Fat: 4 gm	Dietary Fiber: 2 gm
Saturated Fat: 2 gm	Carbs: 60 gm	Sodium: 232 mg
Component of Fat: 11%	Cholesterol: 23 mg	Calcium: 68 mg

Chocolate Raspberry Torte

SERVES 12

6 eggs, separated
1¼ cups sugar
¾ cup breadcrumbs,
    (coarse, not fine)
1½ cups unsweetened
    grated chocolate
1 teaspoon vanilla
½ cup chopped almonds
½ teaspoon double-acting
    baking powder
1½ cups raspberry jam
1 cup raspberries, fresh
    or frozen, defrosted
    and drained

Preheat oven to 325°. Have all ingredients at room temperature. Beat egg yolks until light and lemony color. Gradually beat sugar into yolks. Add breadcrumbs, 1 cup grated chocolate, vanilla, almonds and baking powder.

In a separate bowl, beat egg whites until stiff, and gently fold into batter. Pour into a 9-inch spring-form or tube pan that's been sprayed with non-stick oil, so cake can be removed without much handling. Bake 1 hour, chill, and then remove torte from pan.

Carefully slice cake into two layers. Slide thin flat platter between layers to lift off upper layer. Melt raspberry jam in small saucepan over low heat. Spread one-third of the jam over top of bottom layer. Sprinkle ½ cup chocolate over jam. Replace top layer on cake. Spread remaining jam over top and sides. Arrange raspberries on top. Chill before serving.

Serving: 1/12 Recipe	Calories: 315	Protein: 6 gm
Calories from Fat: 88	Total Fat: 10 gm	Dietary Fiber: 3 gm
Saturated Fat: 3.5 gm	Carbs: 56 gm	Sodium: 112 mg
Component of Fat: 26%	Cholesterol: 106 mg	Calcium: 57 mg

Gingerbread People

*My niece, Amanda, would be truly distraught
if "Gingerbread" was an exclusive men's club.*

$^1/_4$ cup canola oil
$^1/_2$ cup sugar
$^1/_2$ cup dark molasses
$3^1/_2$ cups all-purpose flour
1 teaspoon baking soda
$^1/_4$ teaspoon cloves
$^1/_2$ teaspoon cinnamon
2 teaspoons ginger
pinch of salt
$^1/_4$ cup water

MAKES EIGHT 5" TALL PEOPLE

Preheat oven to 350°. Spray cookie sheet with non-stick oil.

Using electric beater, blend oil, sugar and molasses. Sift flour, then resift with remaining dry ingredients. Mix flour mixture into wet mixture in three parts, alternating each addition with one-third of the water. Roll dough on a lightly floured surface, about $^1/_4$ inch thick. Cut out gingerbread people with cookie cutter or knife. Set on cookie sheet. Use raisins or candied fruits for features and buttons. Bake until dough springs back when lightly pressed, about 8-10 minutes.

Serving: 1 Person	Calories: 341	Protein: 5 gm
Calories from Fat: 67	Total Fat: 7.5 gm	Dietary Fiber: 2 gm
Saturated Fat: .5 gm	Carbs: 64 gm	Sodium: 185 mg
Component of Fat: 20%	Cholesterol: 0 mg	Calcium: 188 mg

Decorating Gingerbread People: For each icing color, blend together $^1/_4$ cup powdered sugar, a few drops of vanilla, water, and 1-2 drops food coloring into a paste. Apply icing with a small knife. To add detail and texture, use a wooden toothpick. (This recipe can also be used to construct Gingerbread Houses.)

New Hampshire Maple Curls

1¼ cups maple syrup
5 tablespoons canola oil
1 cup all-purpose flour
pinch of salt

MAKES THIRTY 3-INCH CURLS

Preheat oven to 350°. Spray cookie sheet with non-stick oil.

Boil maple syrup and oil together for 2 minutes. Remove from heat, stir in flour and salt until well blended.

Drop dough by the tablespoon onto cookie sheet, leaving 3 inches between them. Bake 9-12 minutes, until cookie is the color of maple syrup. Remove pan from oven and let cool 1 minute, then remove cookies one at a time. Place handle of wooden spoon on edge of cookie and roll into a curl around handle.

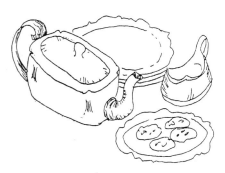

Serving: 1 Curl	Calories: 66	Protein: 0 gm
Calories from Fat: 21	Total Fat: 2.5 gm	Dietary Fiber: 0 gm
Saturated Fat: 0 gm	Carbs: 11 gm	Sodium: 5 mg
Component of Fat: 31%	Cholesterol: 0 mg	Calcium: 16 mg

Berry Cream Custard

1 cup frozen berries
   (strawberries,
   raspberries or
   blueberries)
2 cups skim milk
$^3/_4$ cup honey
pinch of salt
2 beaten eggs
$^1/_2$ teaspoon vanilla
$^1/_2$ cup sugar

SERVES 4

Preheat oven to 300°. Spray 5 individual custard cups with non-stick oil.

Set berries to drain in sieve and reserve juice. In a saucepan on medium heat, blend milk, honey and salt, and scald milk. Remove from heat, whisk in eggs and vanilla. Pour custard filling into prepared cups. Place cups in deep-dish baking pan, then fill baking pan with $1^1/_2$ inches of very hot (not boiling) water. Bake 50 minutes. Chill custard cups.

Boil reserved berry juice with sugar for 10 minutes. Remove from heat, stir in berries. Spoon berry sauce over cooled custard cups.

Serving: 1/4 Recipe	Calories: 381	Protein: 8 gm
Calories from Fat: 26	Total Fat: 3 gm	Dietary Fiber: 1 gm
Saturated Fat: 1 gm	Carbs: 86 gm	Sodium: 127 mg
Component of Fat: 6%	Cholesterol: 108 mg	Calcium: 173 mg

Spiced Bread Pudding

3 cups of ¹/₂-inch cubed
    stale bread
³/₄ cup raisins, dried
    apples or other fruit
3 eggs
³/₄ cup sugar
pinch of salt
12 oz. can skimmed
    evaporated milk
¹/₂ cup very hot (but not
    boiling) water
1 teaspoon cinnamon
¹/₂ teaspoon nutmeg
2 teaspoons vanilla
    extract

SERVES 4

Preheat oven to 350°. Spray 2-quart baking dish with non-stick oil.

Put bread cubes in baking dish and cover with raisins or other dried fruit.

In a mixing bowl, beat together eggs, sugar, salt and milk. Slowly beat in the hot water, cinnamon, nutmeg and vanilla. Pour liquid mixture over bread and fruit.

Bake bread pudding until light golden on top, about 45 minutes. Tastes best served warm.

Serving: 1/4 Recipe	Calories: 457	Protein: 15 gm
Calories from Fat: 53	Total Fat: 6 gm	Dietary Fiber: 2 gm
Saturated Fat: 2 gm	Carbs: 88 gm	Sodium: 317 mg
Component of Fat: 11%	Cholesterol: 163 mg	Calcium: 331 mg

Rum-Ricotta Cheesecake

Cheesecake Crust:
2 cups sugared graham
    cracker crumbs
2 tablespoons canola oil

Cheesecake Filling:
4 eggs
1 cup sugar
1 teaspoon vanilla extract
2 tablespoons rum
8 oz. softened non-fat
    cream cheese
$1^1/_2$ cups part-skim
    Ricotta cheese, well
    drained in sieve
2 tablespoons chopped
    pecans
1 teaspoon flour

MAKES 9-INCH CHEESECAKE

Preheat oven to 300°. Spray 9-inch spring-form pan with non-stick oil.

Combine crust ingredients in mixing bowl. Press cracker crumb mixture into bottom of pan and $2^1/_2$ inches up sides. Bake for 3 minutes, then chill.

In a mixing bowl, beat eggs until light and foamy. Gradually add sugar, vanilla and rum. Add cream cheese and Ricotta, blend until smooth. Dust pecans with flour, stir into filling and pour into crust. Bake 35-40 minutes. Chill 6 hours before serving.

Serving: 1/12 Cheesecake	Calories: 270	Protein: 10 gm
Calories from Fat: 84	Total Fat: 9.5 gm	Dietary Fiber: 1 gm
Saturated Fat: 3 gm	Carbs: 35 gm	Sodium: 277 mg
Component of Fat: 31%	Cholesterol: 82 mg	Calcium: 134 mg

Chocolate Sugar Plums

Choose a crisp dry day for working with chocolate, and work in a temperature of about 70° with no drafts.

1 cup dried apricots,
    finely chopped
1 cup golden raisins
$1/_2$ cup dried currants
1 cup candied orange or
    lemon peel, cherries,
    and other dried or
    glazed fruits
$1/_2$ cup walnuts or
    pecans, finely ground
1 teaspoon cinnamon
4 tablespoons honey
3 tablespoons rum,
    brandy or water
1 lb. milk or semisweet
    chocolate squares

NOTE: You can make Plain Sugar Plums by rolling the fruit balls in sugar instead of dipping them in chocolate.

MAKES 24 SUGAR PLUMS

In a large mixing bowl, combine dried and glazed fruits, nuts, cinnamon and honey. Add just enough liquor or water to make the mixture slightly sticky. Roll and compress into $1^{1}/_{2}$-inch balls. Set balls on wax paper, where they can adjust to a temperature of 70°.

Boil water in lower pan of double boiler. In the top pan, slowly melt chocolate. When chocolate reaches 100° on a candy thermometer, stir constantly. Heat until chocolate reaches 130°, remove from heat and cool to 88°. Adjust burner so water in bottom pan maintains a temperature of 90°. Return chocolate in top pan to double boiler.

Using candy-dipping fork or small slotted spoon dip sugar plums into chocolate. Set on wire rack (with pan below to catch, melt and reuse drippings.) As chocolate begins to harden, set on wax paper to smooth bottoms.

Serving: 1 Sugar Plum	Calories: 181	Protein: 2 gm
Calories from Fat: 58	Total Fat: 7.5 gm	Dietary Fiber: 3 gm
Saturated Fat: 3.5 gm	Carbs: 30 gm	Sodium: 2 mg
Component of Fat: 33%	Cholesterol: 0 mg	Calcium: 10 mg

Seasonal
Preserves & Jams

CONTENTS

ABOUT CANNING

Jars: Use only properly sealed canning jars with rubber airtight seals or a two-piece metal screw-down lid. Check against defects such as chips or cracks. Jars must be sterilized in boiling water or dishwasher, and filled while still hot.

Packing Jars: Fill while preserves and jar are very hot, leaving $1/4$ to $1/2$-inch headroom. Before sealing, release trapped air by running a butter knife or spatula down the insides of the jar. Wipe top of jar clean before sealing.

Canning at a High Altitude: Increase processing time in boiling water bath by 1 minute for every 1000 feet above sea level.

Citrus Marmalade

1 large grapefruit
3 large oranges
2 lemons
10 cups water
7 cups sugar

MAKES ABOUT 16 JELLY JARS

Scrub fruit well. Halve and discard seeds. Scoop pulp into saucepan, then grate in the rind. Add water and let set for 12 hours.

Boil fruit and water mixture for 20 minutes. Refrigerate another 12 hours.

Return to stove and warm mixture on low heat. Add sugar and stir until dissolved. Raise heat to moderate, and cook until 222° is reached on a candy thermometer.

Pour into hot sterilized jars. Seal jars according to manufacturer's directions.

Serving: 2 Tablespoons	Calories: 45	Protein: 0 gm
Calories from Fat: 0	Total Fat: 0 gm	Dietary Fiber: 0 gm
Saturated Fat: 0 gm	Carbs: 12 gm	Sodium: 1 mg
Component of Fat: 0%	Cholesterol: 0 mg	Calcium: 2 mg

Currant Jelly

4 lbs. fresh currants,
    any color or variety
3 cups sugar
1 pouch (3 oz.) liquid
    fruit pectin

MAKES 3 JELLY JARS

Wash currants, but you don't need to trim the stems. Put in a large saucepan, and crush some of the fruit. Cook on low heat for 5 minutes. Raise heat to moderate and cook 25 minutes more.

Strain and squeeze juice through a fine sieve or jelly bag. Return juice to saucepan and add sugar and pectin. Stir constantly while sugar dissolves. Continue to cook until liquid boils for 3 minutes.

Pour into hot sterilized jars. Seal according to manufacturers directions.

Serving: 2 Tablespoons	Calories: 154	Protein: 1 gm
Calories from Fat: 1	Total Fat: 0 gm	Dietary Fiber: 3 gm
Saturated Fat: 0 gm	Carbs: 39 gm	Sodium: 1 mg
Component of Fat: 1%	Cholesterol: 0 mg	Calcium: 25 mg

An herbal cough syrup: Pour 1 cup boiling water over 2 tablespoons of dried sweet cicely and steep for 30 minutes. Combine 2 tablespoons of this tea with 2 tablespoons honey and 1 tablespoon lemon juice.

Apple Butter

*For the best flavor, use McIntosh, Jonathan,
Golden Delicious or other good-cooking apple varieties.*

4 lbs. apples
1 cup water
1 cup cider vinegar
1$\frac{1}{2}$ cups brown sugar
1 teaspoon cloves
2 teaspoons allspice
1 teaspoon finely grated
   lemon rind
2 teaspoons lemon juice

MAKES 5 PINTS

Clean and quarter apples. Cook slowly in water and vinegar for 35 minutes. Drain off liquid and press apple pulp through a strainer. Discard skin and seeds.

Mix pulp with remaining ingredients. Return to pan and cook over low heat for 25 minutes, stirring constantly to keep from sticking. Apple butter is done when a small amount placed on a plate shows no rim of liquid separating from the butter.

Pour into hot sterilized jars. Seal jars according to manufacturer's directions.

Serving: 2 Tablespoons	Calories: 29	Protein: 0 gm
Calories from Fat: 1	Total Fat: 0 gm	Dietary Fiber: 0 gm
Saturated Fat: 0 gm	Carbs: 8 gm	Sodium: 2 mg
Component of Fat: 2%	Cholesterol: 0 mg	Calcium: 5 mg

Winter Fruit Conserve

MAKES 8 CUPS

1 lemon
1 orange
3 pears
3 apples, red or green
2 cups cranberries
1 cup raisins
2 cups honey
$^1/_2$ cup orange juice
2 cups brown sugar
1 tablespoon cinnamon
1 teaspoon ginger
$^1/_2$ cup chopped walnuts

Prepare the fruit as follows and put in a large pot: Cut lemon and orange in half, remove seeds and scoop pulp into pot. Cut unpeeled pears and apples into bite-sized pieces, add to pot with whole cranberries, raisins, honey, orange juice, sugar and spices.

Bring to a boil for 2 minutes. Reduce heat and simmer until temperature reaches 220° on a candy thermometer, about 45 minutes. Add walnuts and pack in hot sterilized jars.

Will keep in refrigerator for 1 week, or seal lid according to manufacturer's directions.

Serving: 2 Tablespoons	Calories: 101	Protein: 2 gm
Calories from Fat: 6	Total Fat: .5 gm	Dietary Fiber: 2 gm
Saturated Fat: 0 gm	Carbs: 24 gm	Sodium: 4 mg
Component of Fat: 6%	Cholesterol: 0 mg	Calcium: 20 mg

Lemon Curd

My favorite spread on toast, biscuits or waffles. Enjoy!

1 cup sugar
3 eggs
2 egg yolks
$^3/_8$ cup lemon juice
1 teaspoon cornstarch
4 tablespoons melted
    butter
4 tablespoons finely
    grated lemon rind

MAKES 1$^1/_2$ CUPS

Combine sugar, eggs and egg yolks in a small bowl. Beat with electric beater for 2 minutes, then beat in lemon juice and cornstarch.

Pour mixture into saucepan. Cook over medium heat, stirring constantly, for 10 minutes or until thickened.

Return cooked mixture to bowl and beat briefly. Continue to beat while gradually adding melted butter and grated lemon rind. Place curd into jars and cover with plastic. Chill and store in refrigerator, where curd will firm. Lemon curd will keep about a month.

Serving: 1 Tablespoon	Calories: 66	Protein: 1 gm
Calories from Fat: 28	Total Fat: 3 gm	Dietary Fiber: 0 gm
Saturated Fat: 1.5 gm	Carbs: 9 gm	Sodium: 29 mg
Component of Fat: 41%	Cholesterol: 50 mg	Calcium: 7 mg

Mostarda

This 4-pint recipe makes extra for holiday gift-giving.
Mustard-fruit preserves will keep in the refrigerator about 2 months.

2 cups sugar
4 cups water
6 inches cinnamon sticks
15 whole cloves
1 teaspoon ground mace
15 peppercorns
2 cups dried apricots
6 dried pineapple rings,
    cut in quarters
1/4 cup currants or raisins
1 lb. fresh chestnuts, in
    the shell
4 cans unsweetened pear
    halves
1 tablespoon dry mustard
3 tablespoons water
1/4 cup whole mustard seed

MAKES 4 PINTS

In a large pot over medium-low heat, dissolve sugar in water. Tie cinnamon, cloves, mace and peppercorns in a cheesecloth, then place bag in the syrup. Simmer 15 minutes. Stir in apricots, pineapple quarters, and currants or raisins. Simmer 40 minutes more. Remove spice bag from sauce.

Put a cross in the flat side of the chestnuts and roast in 375° oven for 10 minutes. Peel chestnuts, chop in quarters and add to sauce. Drain and quarter pears, add to sauce. Stir occasionally and cook 10 minutes more.

Mix dry mustard with 3 tablespoons water, add to sauce. In an ungreased skillet, toast mustard seeds over medium heat, stirring until they pop (about 3 minutes). Mix seeds into mostarda. Seal in hot sterilized jars.

Serving: 1/4 Cup	Calories: 136	Protein: 2 gm
Calories from Fat: 9	Total Fat: 1 gm	Dietary Fiber: 2 gm
Saturated Fat: 0 gm	Carbs: 32 gm	Sodium: 5 mg
Component of Fat: 6%	Cholesterol: 0 mg	Calcium: 19 mg

Pickled Cauliflower

2 lbs. cauliflower florets
   (heads 2-3 inches
   round, with about
   2 inches of stalk)
$1/4$ cup pickling salt
3 cups boiling water
$1^1/_2$ cups vinegar
2 cups water
1 teaspoon sugar
1 bay leaf
1 teaspoon mustard seed
8 peppercorns

MAKES 4 PINTS
Read about canning on page 150.

Put salt and cauliflower in boiling water. Simmer 10 minutes, drain. Pack cauliflower in sterilzed jars. Boil remaining ingredients together 5 minutes and pour over cauliflower, leaving $1/_2$-inch headroom. Seal jars.

Place jars on rack in boiler half-filled with boiling water, with space between jars. Add boiling water to cover jars 2 inches above their tops. Bring to a boil, cover and process 15 minutes. Using tongs, lift jars (not by the lids) and set on towels with several inches between them to cool.

Serving: 1/4 Cup	Calories: 9	Protein: 1 gm
Calories from Fat: 1	Total Fat: 0 gm	Dietary Fiber: 1 gm
Saturated Fat: 0 gm	Carbs: 2 gm	Sodium: 41 mg
Component of Fat: 12%	Cholesterol: 0 mg	Calcium: 6 mg

By around 10,000 B.C., in the Near East and Asia, men had specialized their knowledge in the ways of animals, and women in the ways of plants. The historical record indicates these women were the first farmers, who studied and cultivated the natural tendencies of plants and their propagational preferences.

Pepper-Onion Chutney

6 sweet colored peppers,
    chopped fine
6 green peppers,
    chopped fine
6 large onions,
    chopped fine
4 tomatoes, skinned,
    seeded and finely
    chopped
1 quart vinegar
1 teaspoon pickling salt
1/2 cup honey
1 teaspoon mustard
    powder
1 teaspoon celery seed

MAKES TWO 1-POUND JARS
Read about canning on page 150

Combine all ingredients and bring to a boil. Simmer until somewhat thickened, about 45 minutes. Pack in hot sterilized jars, leaving 1/2-inch headroom in each. Seal jars.

Place jars on rack in boiler half-filled with boiling water, leaving space between them. Add boiling water to cover jars 2 inches above their tops. Bring to a boil, cover, process 15 minutes. Using tongs, lift jars (not by the lids) and set on towels with several inches between them to cool.

Serving: 2 Tablespoons
Calories from Fat: 2
Saturated Fat: 0 gm
Component of Fat: 3%

Calories: 44
Total Fat: 0 gm
Carbs: 11 gm
Cholesterol: 0 mg

Protein: 1 gm
Dietary Fiber: 1 gm
Sodium: 77 mg
Calcium: 13 mg

Eggnog

2 eggs, separated
2 tablespoons sugar
1 cup skim milk
$\frac{1}{4}$ cup non-fat powdered milk
$\frac{1}{4}$ cup rum, brandy or whisky
pinch of ground nutmeg (optional)

SERVES 2

Beat egg yolks until light. Slowly beat in sugar, milk, powdered milk and liquor.

In a separate bowl, whip egg whites until stiff. Gently fold egg whites into eggnog mixture and serve in punch glasses. If desired, sprinkle with nutmeg.

Serving: 1/2 Recipe	Calories: 265	Protein: 13 gm
Calories from Fat: 48	Total Fat: 5.5 gm	Dietary Fiber: 0 gm
Saturated Fat: 1.5 gm	Carbs: 24 gm	Sodium: 173 mg
Component of Fat: 18%	Cholesterol: 216 mg	Calcium: 280 mg

The Coastal New England Cooking Series

NOTES ON USING THESE BOOKS

Each book is oriented to take advantage of the fresh produce of the season. Try to buy locally grown produce in the freshest condition possible. Locally grown food not only has the best flavor and greatest amount of vitamins, but it is economical as well.

To allow for a variety of foods, fruits and vegetables which freeze or dry well are also used in their preferred state of storage. Fresh produce, fish, grains, flours, dairy and beans provide a diverse and healthy diet, without the animal fats and problems associated with red meat.

Non-fat and low-fat dairy products are readily available and provide calcium, protein, nutrition and flavor, with much less fat. They are an excellent substitute for whole milk products. Low-sodium tomato products and bouillon broth are occasionally used, substitution of regular items will simply increase sodium.

Non-stick oil spray is intended to mean a non-fat vegetable oil spray. When it is used in addition to a cooking oil, it allows the use of less oil.

The nutritional analysis assumes a "pinch of salt" or "salt to taste" is .05 teaspoons of salt. The same measurement is used for other spices as well.

Preheating the oven or broiler takes only 15 minutes. Save electricity, don't warm your appliances until 15 minutes before they will be used.

COASTAL NEW ENGLAND   WINTERFARE COOKING

Following the Guidelines of
The American Heart Association

A complete statement of the Guidelines of the American Heart Association can be obtained by contacting your local chapter. For healthy adults, this cookbook presents a simple approach to following these guidelines. Adding together the various nutritional components of your meals will help provide a better understanding of your diet.

By reducing meat and chicken, a large amount of saturated fat (an artery-damaging fat) will be replaced by more healthful protein and fats. Saturated fats should be limited to 10% of calories. All animal products, including cheese, also contain cholesterol, and their use should be limited.

Polyunsaturated fats (found in salmon, leafy vegetables and seeds), and especially the Omega-3 fatty acids, are believed to have an anticlotting agent helpful in preventing heart attack and stroke. Monounsaturated fats are often praised for not raising the damaging LDL cholesterol, and are found in olive and canola oils.

Keep the amount of pre-prepared foods to a minimum. Enjoy a wide variety of fresh foods with a broad range of their natural vitamins, minerals and nutrients. Fresh fruits and vegetables can be eaten regularly, without restriction.

Total fat intake should not exceed 30% of the calories consumed. Even polyunsaturated and monounsaturated fats should be consumed in limited quantities, and will achieve the greatest benefit if they replace, not supplement, the saturated fats presently consumed.

COASTAL NEW ENGLAND   WINTERFARE COOKING

Following the Guidelines of
The American Heart Association

(cont.) Carbohydrates should make up at least 50-60% of the diet. This includes vegetables, fruits, grains, flours and beans. The American Heart Association recommends calories be adjusted to achieve and maintain a healthy body weight.

Make a habit of reaching for fruit or naturally sweetened products. The recipes in this book offer a reasonable alternative to the traditional high-fat and high-calorie desserts, but they are not intended to be eaten every day or in volumes greater than the portions shown.

Sodium intake should follow the advice of your physician, or be limited to an average of 3 grams per day. Recipes in this book can be made without salt or allow for "salt to taste." The desire for salty foods is acquired; you can become more sensitive to the taste of salt by slowly reducing its volume.   Try using sea salt in small amounts. It is more flavorful and contains minerals not present in table salt.

Limit alcohol to a maximum of one or two drinks per day.   And...

Exercise! It makes your body work better, and feel better, too.

Suggested Kitchen Tools, Utensils and Stock Items

Kitchen Tools and Utensils:
Set of whisks in assorted sizes
Slotted spoon and spatula
Blender
Double boiler
Non-stick skillet and frying pans in assorted sizes with lids
Oven casseroles with lids
Non-aluminum pots, pans and containers
Rolling pin
Large stainless steel bowl for mixing bread doughs
Pie pans, regular and deep-dish

Stock Items:
A good variety of spices, fresh fruits and vegetables
Non-stick, non-fat vegetable oil spray
Canola, olive and safflower oils
Vegetable bouillon cubes or powder
Skim milk
Non-fat powdered milk (to enrich skim milk)
Low-fat buttermilk
Non-fat plain yogurt, cottage cheese and cream cheese
Low-fat and part-skim cheese products

Measurements

a pinch.................................. $^1/_{20}$ teaspoon
3 teaspoons............................. 1 tablespoon
4 tablespoons......................... $^1/_4$ cup
16 tablespoons........................ 1 cup
2 cups................................... 1 pint
4 cups................................... 1 quart
4 quarts................................ 1 gallon
8 quarts................................ 1 peck
16 ounces............................. 1 pound
8 ounces liquid....................... 1 cup
1 ounce liquid........................ 2 tablespoons

Substitutions

1 tablespoon cornstarch............ 2 T. flour or 2 tsp. quick-cooking tapioca
2 teaspoons arrowroot.............. 1 tablespoon cornstarch
1 teaspoon baking powder.......... $^1/_4$ tsp. baking soda + $^1/_2$ tsp. cream of tartar
$^1/_2$ cup brown sugar.................. 2 T. molasses in $^1/_2$ cup granulated sugar
$^3/_4$ cup cracker crumbs.............. 1 cup bread crumbs
1 tablespoon fresh herbs........... 1 teaspoon dried herbs
1 small clove garlic.................. $^1/_8$ teaspoon garlic powder
1 fresh onion......................... 2 T. instant minced onion, rehydrated
1 cup whole milk..................... $^1/_2$ c. skimmed evaporated milk + $^1/_2$ c. water
1 cup buttermilk...................... 1 cup non-fat plain yogurt

COASTAL NEW ENGLAND   WINTERFARE COOKING

167

PRINTED IN THE U.S.A.

20% TOTAL RECYCLED FIBER
20% POST CONSUMER FIBER

If you enjoy this seasonal cookbook, try the others in the Coastal New England Cooking series. Each book has 180 pages of great New England recipes, historical and culinary trivia, and the original artwork of local artists. Our unique and beautiful covers complement the flavor of this wonderful collection. Cookbooks are also a gift that will be used for years.

_____ *Coastal New England Spring Cooking*..........................$13.95

_____ *Coastal New England Summertime Cooking*.................$13.95

_____ *Coastal New England Fall Harvest Cooking*................$13.95

_____ *Coastal New England Winterfare & Holiday Cooking*...$13.95

_____ Total Quantity x $13.95.....................$_____

Maine Residents add 6% sales tax...........$_____

Shipping Charge: $2.00 first book, $_____
plus $1.00 for each additional book

TOTAL $_____

Please enclose check or money order made payable to:

Harvest Hill Press
P.O. Box 55
Salisbury Cove, Maine 04672

VISA / M.C # __ __ __ __ - __ __ __ __ - __ __ __ __ - __ __ __ __

Expiration Date:_____   Signature_____

For faster service on VISA / Master Card orders, call (207) 288-8900.

Orders paid by personal check shipped within 3 weeks of receipt,
all other orders shipped in 3 business days.